I, Jeanne Guyon

I, Jeanne Guyon

by Nancy Carol James, Ph.D.

James, Ph.D., Nancy C.
I, Jeanne Guyon / Nancy C. James, Ph.D.
ISBN 978-0-9778033-9-2

Printed in the United States of America

Published by:
SeedSowers
Christian Books Publishing House
PO Box 3317
Jacksonville, FL 32206
(800) 228-2665

www.SeedSowers.com

Table of Contents

PUBLISHER'S NOTE

Jeanne Guyon's daughter had the same name, Jeanne. The author of this book wanted to avoid confusion and misunderstanding that would arise from both having the same name. For that reason, she has called the daughter Anne-Marie. Her real name was Jeanne-Marie.

SeedSowers Publishing

Prologue

Life goes by so quickly. I know that now, and really have known it my whole life. I want my short time on this earth to be spent serving God, and I know that relating to God takes every second we have in this world. Somehow from the beginning of my life, I, the greatest of sinners, could see that only one thing mattered to me: pleasing God and living in the beautiful power of His Spirit.

You see, I believe in the presence of Jesus Christ gracing my life with wonder, and I sought this beautiful love my whole life. Truly I, Jeanne Guyon, would have been happy living in a closet where Jesus spent time with me. How can I say this? Jesus Christ, the Son of God, pours his Spirit into us, and I, unworthy sinner, have been one of many who receive it. My wisdom is Jesus, plain and simple.

I lived in a time of history, though, when the Christians who believed in the personal power of the Spirit were held in contempt; and, sadly, my belief that Jesus lives within me brought me serious problems. As the Gospel says in Matthew 10:18, I was brought before kings and governors for the sake of Jesus. Yet, even with everything that happened, I lived the simple faith of relating to Jesus Christ; and, if I had to do it all over again, I would make the same decision. Live Jesus! Love Jesus! And fulfillment beyond our wildest imagining fills our hearts and souls.

I
My Home in Montargis

I, Jeanne Guyon, write this with my own hand. I was born in the small French town of Montargis, surrounded by the famous medieval Forest of Paucourt. My home town lay on the River Loire, the longest river in France, and had sheltered French royalty for centuries. Crisscrossed by canals, Montargis was proud to be close to Orléans, the home of Joan of Arc. The Loire River, the river of kings, flowed close to our house with its awesome beauty, its rushing water and lovely swishing sound of the waves.

I was born into a troubled family. Both of my parents had children from first marriages, and we never found a peaceful unity in our family, even though my family was one of destiny. My ancestors led and ruled society and knew strong connections to royalty, but not the royalty of brutal power and gambling that sadly entered into the French court. We were the royalty of looking at this glorious creation and desiring to serve the living Lord; someone in our lineage had learned to raise interior eyes from the gifts of life to the Giver of it all. They had known that every human carried an amazing gift, a soul, and that this soul yearned for connection with God. The Lord wants all of us to feel the divine power poured into our soul—and then know the transcendent joy of purpose and motion and love.

In 1648 I was born premature, weak, and seemingly dying, and was baptized as soon as I was born. After my birth, many times the doctors thought they were losing me, a tiny, fragile girl. I was sick until I was three years old, but even then I wanted to live. From the start, I struggled to live and in my battles with death, I sensed the fresh and amazing vision of life lived in Christ.

The Nursery

Torn apart by rushes of pain, of great swelling in my leg, I began to recognize a woman coming in and, with tears dripping from her eyes, holding my weak little hand. I saw large tears, unnoticed by the woman, falling upon my nose and splattering, and then more tears swishing onto my fingers. I tried to respond to her hand but noticed no change on her face. The patter of tears upon me became my comfort.

The doctor spoke to the woman, my mother, "Madame, the little girl might not make it. So weak, and with the wound on her leg." He checked his language to avoid saying how repulsive the open wound looked on such a young child. He saw the pace of the mother's tears quicken and he said quietly, "Who are we to say who should live or die?"

My mother Jeanne le Maistre de la Maisonfort, answered, "When I was pregnant with her, I had a great shock." She stopped as if reluctant, but then continued: "I opened the door and it was a young man—a strange man dressed all in brown with a green hat and eyes matching the strange garb on his brown hair."

The doctor sighed: not superstitious about the forest people from Paucourt, the forest surrounding Montargis! But then, drumming his fingers upon the sick girl's bed, he looked up and saw the crying mother's open eyes. From their luminous quality vital sparks of life flew out.

He questioned, "What did he say?"

"Nothing. He stared at my large bulging stomach, then he turned and left as quickly as he came. And I fell and felt kicking within me as if she herself wanted to live. They led me to bed and it took days to feel"—she decided upon honesty—"to feel anything again. Soon this sick child entered our sad world."

The doctor looked away. As much as he scorned the words of these forest people, he recognized power, at least for the worried mother.

Carefully, as he backed out of the room, the doctor confessed, "I know not whether she shall live or die."

Her familiar face, looming over me, smiled and I tried again to let her know I was here, pushing hand against hand. My mother threw her head back and laughed. "Good girl! A squeeze! You are alive there!"

A man, my father, Claude Bouvier de la Mothe, walked in to peer at me. Caressing my hand, he whispered, "Welcome, little mademoiselle!" He backed slowly out, staring at the young girl as if to remember forever this moment.

I lived. Even then I wanted to be part of the adventure of life. Yet, our family feuded and fought, and I never had a place to belong.

With my family connections, I never knew who would be visiting at our home. When I was eight, a queen came to visit.

"Who is that girl? That beauty with the eyes?" I heard an older woman ask.

"Her name is Jeanne and what an unusual one."

I ran over and looked into the grey-haired woman's glowing eyes, whom they call Queen Henriette Marie de France, the queen consort of England.

"You are important to God!" I exclaimed.

Silence happened and I knew some power was present. Something like a wave of beauty had been knocked out of me and for an instant I wanted to run away. I overheard the intense murmured conversation.

The queen insisted, "Let me take this child back to England to my court. I will keep her close to me and have her trained for a royal position."

My father walked over and put his arm on my mother's shoulder, "My Jeanne, darling, our little Jeanne will have the world open in front of her if we let her go. She might thank us for this one day after she takes the splendid position that the Queen will prepare for her. Yet, I cannot bear to part with her."

My mother looked at me. "Jeanne must stay with us." I stared at my crying mother and, walking over, hugged her legs.

Then laughter filled the cavernous room and echoed around the pillars as the queen said, "The little girl has decided. Let her stay, but remember, something special will happen to her, whether she is at my royal court or in your beautiful home. We shall speak of this no more."

As I looked at my mother, I saw a new color in her eyes, the raw shade of fear and wonder: who was this child who knew how to speak for herself even now.

Even with her declaration of love for me, my mother kept working constantly at the local parish. After that, all I remembered is the aloneness of it all, surrounded by yelling and then stony silences. I remember walking around the large house for hours without relief, wondering when I would meet up with someone.

My Childhood

I grew up passed from servant to servant. When my father noticed I was neglected, he found religious houses to take me in and give me an education. At the age of three, I lived with the Ursuline Sisters, was brought home for a few months, and sent to the Dominicans from age four to six. After a short time at home, I was back at the Ursulines from age six to ten. I learned to read well and spent time with two older half-sisters who were nuns.

When living at home, I was alone. At the age of ten, I carried my favorite doll to show to my mother who was busy getting ready to go to church. "See, Mama," I said. "I braided Anne's hair."

My mother glanced at the doll's braided yarn hair. "And did it incorrectly," she chided. "Go outside and play, Jeanne. I'm on my way to mass."

Slowly I walked towards the door. My brother Guillaume ran in, pushing me out of the way, and grabbed my doll. "Stupid doll!" he yelled. Guillaume ran out of the room, swinging Anne by the recently finished braids.

"Mama! Help me!" I begged.

Instead my mother rebuked, "I told you to leave."

Obediently, eyes now wet, I walked toward the front door. Glancing up, I saw the cross on the wall, with the man hanging on it, his arms and legs sticking out at painful angles, I wondered if the man on the cross cried also.

I found my visiting older half-sister, the nun. Hearing the welcome rustle of Cécile's black robes, I reached over to grab her and she in turn held me in a long, tender hug. Held in her arms, I felt that her black fabric carried a peace all its own. I felt a beautiful heavy sense of God.

I relaxed against her. "My brother won't leave me alone. Everything I do is wrong. He complains about me constantly to Mama and she believes him. And Guillaume beats me. I used to scream for help but now I don't anymore."

Cécile looked at me directly. "Jeanne, I have something to say to you. God loves you very much, but God never tells us to feel sorry for ourselves. Never hide in those weak feelings, Jeanne. Pray for Guillaume when he hurts you."

I felt suddenly hot and words flew out.

"Pray for him! He doesn't deserve that."

Once again, Cécile's steady eyes locked my eyes in a long gaze. "We all have talked to Papa about this, Jeanne. Now you must trust God to show you how to handle this. Come see me often."

Squeezing her hand, I said softly. "Whenever Papa lets me, I will visit."

"Be strong, Jeanne. Have courage."

Looking intensely at her, I ran out of the room, my chest still heaving. Suddenly I saw my father Claude Bouvier de la Mothe walking up the hill toward our mansion. Waving at me, his arm stiffened when he saw my wet face.

He walked over and gently picked up my trembling hand.

"Jeanne, Jeanne, my little girl born later in my life. If I could take the struggles of life away from you, I would. God knows I would."

One of the hunting dogs trailing him came over and started sniffing my shoes, head cocked as he listened to the sound of my tears. Looking intently into my father's face, I started to blurt out ideas.

"My child, silence. I understand. I see how things are with your mother and all of these brothers and sisters. I see you trying to make a way through all this noise and confusion. I am like you in that regard.

"I can only tell you what I know for sure: pray, Jeanne, pray. But don't just wait for God to change things: change yourself. Some parts of life will comfort you, but others…" He sighed. Then my father said an unusual comment. "Use my library. Read the theologians: what an interesting time we live in with all these Christians arguing, some Protestant and others Catholic. Read all of these religious and spiritual thinkers, and the happiness you will find there will dwarf any others in this world."

Even as the words come out, he looked at his pretty child. Wasn't her destiny just to be a beauty and grace some future husband's house? Look at that natural radiance and her rich brown hair! Would a spiritual life ruin her chances for a good marriage? But, despite his doubts, Monsieur de la Mothe continued. "When they tease you or threaten you, my honey child, please run to my library. Do not come to tell me about the injustice. I know the problems in our home better than anyone. Read and study, think and understand. Come to my library and listen to the questions in your mind and heart. Honor them and somehow, God willing, there will be a way for you."

Loud voices rang out from the home as our door was flung open.

"Start now, Jeanne, run!"

I felt the approaching domestic conflicts and quickly bolted for the back door. I saw that my father had given me a new path, a key to wisdom and knowledge. I found a book by John Calvin, whom many talk about in Montargis, and settling in my own father's chair, I began to read. My travel into the infinite had begun.

Peasants in Need

I heard the open conversation between my parents. My father's angry voice carried through the house. "Louis arrests so many that he does not like and sends them to the Bastille. How outlandish and unfair this is: this friend of ours who tried (however imperfectly!) to serve his king—look how he has been treated. Also, Louis has tried to destroy the Fouquet family. The justice of God asks us to continue to welcome them to our home."

My mother responded, "I agree. This is the right thing to do: the children from these oppressed families need a place to call their home. They are always welcome here, even if their fathers are incarcerated."

Soon my parents talked to us: some distressed children and adults will stay with us for safety, and we are never to disclose their real names. I later knew that my parents helped Nicolas Fouquet, Louis' incarcerated Minister of Finance, and his family, as well as others.

Early one morning, I stepped outside and saw peasants walking out of the forest and heading straight to our house. My mother spoke to me as she put on her bonnet. "I am busy today, Jeanne. Many are coming here for food. Go to your room." And my mother moved quickly out of the door, hurrying towards the kitchen. I walked slowly out of the room. What am I to do? Sadly I sat down on the chair next to my small bed. The long day stretched out in front of me, immense and empty. Looking up, I saw the Bible I had borrowed from the library sitting decorously on my dressing table. Why not read the Bible, I thought. Reaching for the book, I opened to the book of Genesis. "In the beginning God created the heavens and earth."

What a wonderful experience in creation, I wondered! A forest-green tree pops out surrounded by yellow flowers, a peacock with a royal-blue breast strolls over there, and sparkling rivers starting to rush in the ecstatic music of the creation. I found my favorite wooden rocking chair and settled down to read.

My First Experience with My Savior

For ensuing months I continued to read through the Bible. I read in the Gospel, Mark 5:25, "The woman with the flow of blood reached out to Jesus. 'If I can touch him,

I will be healed,' the woman thought to herself." I let the Bible drop from my hands and stretched out my own fingers, one by one.

"I will, I must reach out to touch Jesus." I continued reading: "And the woman touched the edge of Jesus' robe. Instantly, her flow of blood stopped. She was healed. Jesus turned around in the crowd, 'Who touched me?'" I turned my head, intent, listening, and my hand relaxed after I hear a door opening in the hallway. I waited to see if my mama was calling me. Yet, only silence. Then I heard the sound of disappearing footsteps. And then more quiet.

The moment had come. Breathing quietly, I again picked up the Bible. "'I touched you, Master,' the woman said in fear." I pressed my palms together. To know and love Jesus, to listen to him, to give him my heart! Oh, Lord, accept me as I am and help me! And somehow I, young Jeanne, knew my life had been accepted by Jesus, my Savior. I had cast my life upon Jesus and, plunging into the sacred waters of his blood, had come out as white as pure wool.

I began to pray regularly in a small chapel on my father's estate dedicated to the miracle of the incarnation of God. I simply said in my own words, "I want to know you well, dear Jesus. Please look upon me with favor and help me.

Give me your love and I give you mine!" A sweet spirit settled on me and I sensed him with me just like he blessed those children in the Gospel long ago. That morning as I sat quietly waiting for breakfast, my mama put a special treat on my plate, a warm blueberry muffin. I sniffed the warm aroma and decide that Jesus would like this, so I pretended to eat it and secreted it away on my lap. After breakfast I walked down to the chapel and offered it to Jesus. A treat for him! I found a nook in the wall where no one would notice and the muffin went in it. Soon I stored a little pile of treats for Jesus, and in my heart I found a larger place for that spiritual sweetness inside that he gave me.

My Conflicted Family Life Continues

At a holiday dinner, in my red lace dress, I walked into the room to see my entire family assembled, with my parents' grown children talking quietly in the dark wood room. A long oblong dining table offered rich cheeses, fresh breads and special fruit cakes. Quickly I looked for my Papa and saw him walking toward me. A member of the ruling council of Montargis, my father leaned over to smile at me, gently stroking my cheek with his index finger.

Father de la Mothe, my older half-brother who was already ordained a Catholic priest, strode over to us, interrupting the greeting.

"Here is our little reader. Do you know, Father, that Jeanne claims to have read the entire Bible? How preposterous to have a girl saying that! And where would she even have gotten this Bible?" His haughty eyes sought his father's eyes which turned toward me.

My father questioned. "Is this true, Jeanne?"

I was pleased to have an answer which I knew would make him proud. "Yes, Papa, I did. Last summer when Mama was busy."

Raising his eyebrows, my brother looked at Papa directly, now ignoring me. "Jeanne must be taught not to lie."

Papa nodded slowly while the young priest walked away. Then Papa looked at me, his intense eyes consuming every detail of what he saw in me.

I barely heard what he whispered. "Be careful what you say, Jeanne."

I let him go no further. "But, Papa, I read the Bible every day. I understand what it says." Then, standing straight, I stretched up to him on my tippy-toes. "Jesus tells me lots of good things when I read!"

His immediate hug offered his only answer. Taking a breath, he continued. "Listen, child. This is a dangerous world. Do not talk to others about God. The Inquisition is everywhere. Do you understand? The Inquisition searches to stop religious heresy, and your idle talk may be punished. Stay quiet, Jeanne." He emphasized every word. "The Church through the Inquisition can arrest people and many have been burned at the stake."

I tried to practice being quiet right then and there. My lips closed in a tight and narrow line.

Looking to each side, he then backed away from me and said in a loud voice, "Go play with your dolls, Jeanne."

I walked around our estate: expansive, filled with beautiful things and good food; many that saw it were jealous. When we went places in our carriage, I knew that some disapproved of my parents, and not because they had wealth and power. My family was what they called controversial, or radical even, because they ministered to the peasants in our area. Peasants, formerly called serfs or slaves, did the farm work and cared for the animals, but most landowners stayed away from them.

I heard tales from my parents talking late at night. My mother spoke rapidly. "The Thirty-Year Religious War with the Treaty of Westphalia ended right after Jeanne was born; but, oh, how these peasants have suffered! We have whole villages starving, and some suffering from the bubonic plague and the soldiers attacking their villages. I cannot bear the sight of these people in pain and, Claude, I am going to help."

My father sighed. "But we are not even supposed to acknowledge these poor ones. Others talk about your work feeding them, and some criticize what you are doing. Yet, I know you are right, and I am," he paused as he swallowed deeply, "proud of you. Still our children need you more than the poor. Just remember them too."

I knew that the previous religious wars, Catholics and Protestants killing each other, had made an unhappy social atmosphere. Now the frequent famines, intensified by the high French taxes and aggressive tax agents, left many peasants gaunt and dying. The agents could show up and take away the cow, the only source of food and the only helper the peasant family would have.

My busy mother swept by me one morning carrying a large tray of food to the door. It smelled wonderful, but I knew it was not for me or even for my family. She opened the door, and I overheard her name said with respect by a crowd waiting. "Madame de la Mothe is here!" "She has brought food!" Peering around my mama, I saw entire hungry families waiting quietly and my mother passing out what she had. I looked up to see tears standing in her eyes. My mother murmured, "The peasants are starving, Jeanne, dying without anyone to help." Then turning quickly, she almost ran back to work in her kitchen. Praying while talking, she said, "As long as I live, I will work to stop this famine." And somehow after saying this, she seemed stronger again and rapidly loaded another tray of food, though she tripped as she pushed on the door. I caught my pretty mama's arm and heard her saying in a low voice, "Merci, my little mademoiselle!" For a brief instant I saw her and she saw me, and I knew that the forces of famine seemed to have destroyed her also: but what should she do? Look away? Or throw herself into the fray and do what she could? Their human need had sunk into her soul and faithfully she tried to help.

Sparkling warmth surrounded me and I vowed, "One day I want to be as kind to the poor as she is."

My Youth and Marriage

I lived with the Dominicans at age ten for an education. My mother brought me home when I was twelve and began to spend time teaching me how to intensify my natural beauty. She prepared me for an active social life, along with a new and elegant wardrobe and hairstyles.

My parents made a decision when I was fifteen years old.

"Who is Jesus to me?" I wondered, as I walked contemplatively through the mysterious forest. We Christians give Jesus allegiance and pledge our loyalty to him. I thought of Cecile's calm, black nun habit and her peace. I imagined me kneeling in the chapel of the nunnery taking vows to Jesus, and I breathed deeply. Then, seeing the sun setting, I headed back home toward all the sounds of my blended family. But soon, I will have the peace of the nunnery: I yearned for the constant praise and prayer, along with work for the poor.

"Jeanne! Come here! Your father has something to tell you."

With the colored light of the setting sun shining on her, my mother stood tall, silhouetted against the polished wood door. I started to run: maybe finally Papa will say yes to my desire to become a nun. Running to his study, I suddenly saw my father's flushed face, with stern arms folded across his chest. He held legal papers in his hands.

"I have decided your future. You will marry our neighbor Jacques in two weeks. You have seen his estate many times. His first wife has been dead for several years now." He looked at me with unusual stormy eyes. "I hope you show gratitude to your mother and me for making such a good marriage."

Suddenly an unnerving quiet filled the room and I heard the blood pounding in my ears.

"No, Papa, no! Why, he is old. And I want to be a nun!"

My father placed his hands over his face and then turned again towards me. "No, daughter. I cannot let this life happen to you. The church is full of treachery, and some of the priests are not decent men. Jacques Guyon is a very wealthy man." Seeing my contorted face, he spoke in a softer tone. "Please, daughter, I beg you. Change your mind. Choose marriage and a family over the religious life. You are the one Monsieur Guyon has chosen, out of many girls who desire this good match."

His pleading awakened some hope in me. "Papa, no. I want to join Cécile's religious order."

He looked away. "I must decide for you. You will be a wife, not a nun."

Blinding tears poured out of my eyes. I reached desperately out for my waiting mother. She also wept.

"Mama! Save me, Mama! No! No!"

Her choked voice became hard. "This is a good marriage, Jeanne. We will dress you beautifully for the ceremony. Jeanne, you will be a rich wife and never know poverty. Thank God for that."

I tried to hug her but she pushed away my trembling body. My mother spoke slowly.

"Jeanne, you know how we talk about the need for water in Paris and our part of France. Monsieur Guyon's father designed and built all the canals around here to bring water from our beautiful rivers. He was a brilliant man. Our king rewarded him richly for this work. Now his son wants you as a wife."

Choking, I begged for her help. "I have never even met him!"

Suddenly my mother grimaced. "You are a beautiful girl. I will explain to you later what will happen in your marriage. In our era, Jeanne, many starve. His money will help; maybe you can work as I do."

And in the next few days, I quietly stood as seamstresses draped lace around me. My mother whispered in my ear what will be expected on the wedding night, and horror filled my being. I, so modest and young, now will marry a man whom I did not know.

Two weeks later on February 18, 1664, I, dressed in antique French lace and a white gown, walked slowly into the Catholic parish where a bishop waited to conduct the marriage ceremony. I saw the strange older man who was soon to be my husband. Glancing over, I looked at my family sitting together in the first pews of the church. Tears dripping uncontrollably, I still wanted to be a nun.

My new husband, Jacques Guyon, leaned over to kiss me, and I stiffened. And now we walked towards the elegant carriage waiting to take us to days of feasting. As we entered our carriage, I noticed the eyes of my half-brother Father de la Mothe intently looking at my new husband, the wealthy Monsieur Jacques Guyon.

II
Married Years

At the age of fifteen I moved into my thirty-eight-year-old husband's mansion which we shared with my mother-in-law Therese. I began to investigate the chests full of antique silver. Picking up an old family teapot, I ran my finger along the decorative engraving. Maybe I will have a tea party. What had St. Paul said about the goodness of hospitality and entertaining?

My mother-in-law walked in. "Put that down immediately. That is only used at holidays."

I froze: rules and tradition everywhere; yet, I leaned against the table and put the teapot down. I started walking towards the quiet closet off our large bedroom. Maybe if I prayed, I would find peace.

I found my formal prayers and read them out loud. I waited. Then I tried more formal devotions and felt increasingly tense as nothing changed. Where was any hope, I wondered. I remembered that hidden blueberry muffin left in my parents' chapel and found a faint smile rising to my face. What a silly and sweet gesture so long ago! Yet now, already married to a man who does not talk to me and with a mother-in-law who does not like me, what could I look forward to? Nothing was sweet anymore.

I knew what the gossip was about me: women murmured, "Poor Jeanne—so young and vibrant and full of divine hope: then sold into a marriage for money and security. And now look at her! Mute and unattractive."

I found no words coming out of my mouth anymore, and no one cared if I should give up talking.

Days went by in my mute state. One winter day I walked into the kitchen and saw a large butcher knife there, and quickly I wanted to grab it and cut my tongue out and leave it here in the kitchen and go bleed to death in my closet. My hand reached toward the knife—what a relief this will be, I decided. I see the sunlight glinting off of the blade—so close and this could all be over. Then in my mind, I saw my father's face smiling at me. "Use my library, Jeanne. How I wish I could save you from this dangerous world!" But the knife seemed almost to call to me. As my hand slid toward it, closer, closer, then I briefly saw in my mind my father in despair, crying in his room. His little Jeanne lost for eternity and he had done this to her! Suddenly finding strength enough to deny this self-mutilation, I backed out of the kitchen, turning my eyes away from the welcoming knife; yet I still longed for an end to this life. Why, oh why, did this have to happen? Why did my parents do this to me? Was I such an awful person that I deserved this misery?

Years continued to pass and I became increasingly unhappy. At age nineteen and pregnant with my second child, I visited my father. Looking at me, Monsieur de la Mothe appeared to have seen a ghost. I knew my beauty no longer sparkled and I did not even care.

"Jeanne, there is a Franciscan brother visiting us today. He has been on a long retreat in silence. Would you like to meet with him?"

I slowly nodded, agreeing to his offer. Papa summoned the brother Archange Enguerrand and left us alone.

I was unused to speaking, but tried to be open. "I cast about for peace, Brother. I pray but my prayers fall short and I never feel different. I attend mass as often as I am allowed."

The Franciscan brother made a surprised sound. "Allowed, Madame?"

I looked down. "Yes, my husband tells me if and when I can attend mass."

The brother sighed. He walked over to the window and looked out at the forest near this mansion.

I continued, "I want to please God, yet I feel so unhappy."

The brother turned and asked softly, "Are you in despair?"

"That is not too strong."

A quiet pause broke this conversation. Then the Franciscan brother turned towards me, words seeming to flood into his consciousness. He looked into my dull eyes. "It is, Madame, because you seek without what you have within. Always seek God in your heart, and you will find God there."

I felt a sudden infusion of love. The words dropped into my heart like a smooth pebble splashing into a peaceful river. God dwelled inside of me. I could live with Christ! I could find him within my heart!

I wrote about this, "The good brother told me about the powerful presence of God—that you read a few sentences about love for God and then you wait in the quiet presence and find tenderness, sympathy, answers, power. I felt refreshed and reinvigorated as I sat waiting for God. It was more than believing that God loved me—it was rushing toward God inside as quickly as a running river flowing down to the ocean."

Daily now I continued my newly discovered way of praying, feeling the attractive Holy Spirit and the loving desire for my Savior Jesus.

Daily I sought God's presence. I sat in my room, waiting for inspiration—waiting, waiting. Time passed, but still I sat. I saw the light shifting upon the floor. And now my time was over. I stood up, still patient. God will not visit me today. Tomorrow I would return, waiting, waiting.

The next day arrived.

Again I walked into my closet to pray. I felt warm light, splendid victory, in my small room. Closing my eyes, my Jesus brought me happiness. With interior prayer, I sat at the feet of Jesus and enjoyed his presence.

Suddenly I heard the scrape of the door opening. Jacques' mother stood there. "This is disgraceful! The servants talk everywhere about my son's wife who prays constantly. Get out immediately!" Dazed at the interruption, I stumbled out of my place of seclusion.

"You are a lazy girl. If you must do something, learn to play cards like the other wives!"

The day wore on as I inwardly prayed. Should I back down from my powerful interior life? I made my decision. That evening I sat down at the dinner table, looking down at my hands clasped together in my lap. Exploding, Jacques yelled at me. "What is this I hear about you praying again during the day? You know I said you are not to do this."

My mother-in-law looked at me contemptuously. "This is all this silly woman thinks about. Jeanne will bring great disgrace on this household. You must do something about this," she demanded of her son. "Everyone knows that Jeanne has an evil spirit. Even her own mother says that. Jeanne must be controlled."

I remained silent, thinking of Christ who came to me when I prayed. Alive, glorious, offering rest, his presence settled on me. My eyes closed at even the thought of this and I experienced the happiness of Christ.

Then to my surprise I quietly spoke up, "I will not give up my prayer. Christ within me encourages me to continue in prayer." And I left the table, not noticing the loud, outraged voices which followed me. Carried away by the wings of love, I flew into the arms of my Savior who gave me everything I need.

For most, the vibrant inner life would have died quickly. Somehow for me, the more the world tried to destroy me, the more I committed myself to the presence of Christ.

I Begin My Ministry

In Louis XIV's France, as the tax rate increased, desperation grew in poor households. I now began to reach out to others in need, something like my own Mama's life. I walked toward my carriage. "I am going to visit Michelle today. Take me there immediately."

The carriage driver sought for assurance about the destination, "The unusual girl with the light yellow hair? But, Madame, with such a young beauty, their family has plenty of food."

"That is what concerns me. Quickly, let us go."

I prayed before we approached the house. What an unusual message I brought to this family blessed by this attractive child.

"Monsieur and Madame, I have come to talk to you about Michelle."

The father and mother stood oddly alert, at the sign of this aristocratic young woman, a vibrant beauty herself, appearing at their hut.

"Michelle must start coming to my house every day and I will teach her how to read and write. She will be in danger, living without skills to support herself."

Stunned, the mother looked at her feet.

I continued, "I need to speak openly. I fear that a man will take Michelle and use her badly. She is a beautiful girl, too attractive, and people are already talking about what will happen to her. Let us doubly protect her against what the world will do to her. I will prepare her for honest work, and if a decent man approaches, an honorable marriage. But with her beauty, one day she may be taken and end up in an illicit place in Paris or Versailles."

Michelle's mother's eyes filled with tears. The father's face reddened and his fists clenched. "Oui, Madame. We will work together so our daughter's life will not be thrown away."

Michelle's tragedy was stopped. When people suffered, I wanted to help them as I had been helped. I had learned that God delighted in our humility, and when we were humble, He filled our hearts with love.

I wanted everyone to know about Christ within, the interior life!

I continued my praying and actively raised my children: first one son, then another son, and a third child, a daughter. But I still experienced an unusual sense of destiny hovering over my life.

I now lived life for Christ and talked to others about Christ, and I loved Him so very, very deeply. One gray, chilly day while visiting Paris, on my way to the Cathedral of Notre Dame, I saw the magnificent cathedral spires surging up to heaven, with sculptures of frightening gargoyles and lively angels at the top. I ran to pray and a beggar quietly moved into my path. My father had told me that some people like this were angels or those gifted with prophecies, and my whole life had trained me to listen to these ones living fully by the Spirit.

The peaceful, elderly beggar said to me, "Madame, I need to have a word with you."

I pulled the veil aside so I could see him directly. "Monsieur, what can I do for you?"

With a look of intent compassion, he began. "I have a word for you from God, because you have a special place with God. Christ asks you to suffer for him and with him, so you find your place in the Kingdom of God."

His eyes spoke almost as much as his words: sparkling, healthy, yet deep beyond all imagining. Somehow, no questions were necessary.

I knew I needed to say yes to this plan. "I accept whatever God wills for me." Immediately the beggar was gone; and slowly now, I walked toward the praise-filled cathedral. I never saw him again, but the anointing Spirit of that brief conversation lasted forever.

Leaving Paris, the next day I returned home to the mansion, still pondering the odd prophecy. I wondered,

"A strange suffering will come upon me? How could this be? I have wealth, beauty, three healthy children, and an active ministry. Yes, I have a strong passion for God that frequently puzzles me and leaves me hungering for God—but suffering that leads to the Kingdom of God. Will the beggar's words come true?" Somehow I did not doubt this—the strangely beautiful timbre of his voice resonated peacefully in my mind and the strong assurance in his eyes carried an authority I had never seen before.

Sharing in the Sufferings of Christ

One day as I moved around preparing for the day's dinner, I glanced at my son. His eyes glowed oddly. I reached for his forehead and felt an unhealthy heat, flushed hot, and quickly I put him to bed.

"Jacques! Send someone to get the doctor! He is sick!"

My husband walked in and looked at the child and then, turning to a servant, barked an order to find the physician.

In the next few hours, I knew increasing panic and terror, yet stopped for a quick prayer. "Christ, help us! Lord, my children, my children, make them well!"

Now my other children also were becoming feverish and hot, calling for a relief that I could not supply.

"Where are you, Mama!"

Trying to calm my trembling voice, I said quietly, "Right here, darling."

"I can't see you! Why is the room on fire? Where are you, Mama! Stop this. Get that old man by the fireplace out of here. Where are you, Mama?"

And with no fireplace in sight, I started the only medicine I knew: singing praise to God.

"Lullaby, and good night, may the angels protect you," I hummed.

"No, Mama! Put the fire out."

Panicking, I waited and waited for what seemed endless hours. When would the doctor come, when would help arrive? Praying, crying out to God, I saw one by one all of my children growing ill, pale, and then red, screaming, crying. My children, my joy, all suffering, crying, but then even worse, one by one they became dreadfully quiet, limp, lifeless.

Christ, where were you?

Finally I heard the welcome sound of a carriage pulling in front of the house. The doctor walked in somberly with few words.

"Take me to them."

Together we rushed up to the nursery bedrooms where the children lay limp. The doctor compassionately inspected them and then turned to speak to me, saying the fearful words, "Madame Guyon, your children have smallpox. You must leave here to save yourself."

I felt tears patter out of my eyes like raindrops, and I knew I must stay. "I will wait upon my children."

I went through days of restless and endless work, wiping them down with cool cloths, watching and waiting for the doctor's daily visit. The fever raged within the small bodies of my beloved children.

One day as I walked into the nursery, I felt odd, blown up like an immense elephant with fire everywhere. A servant heard me fall and ran to help. "Oh, Madame, what happened?" The servant cried, "You are hot! Oh, no. The fever has gotten you too."

Falling into a heap, I heard screaming. Maybe it was me screaming that I cannot desert my children. During the next few days, I tossed in bed, trying to get to my children, and not being able to move, the elephant still sitting on my chest, suffering, hurting, being hot, so very, very hot.

One day, I became aware of someone sitting in my room, entirely dressed in black. Slowly I opened my eyes to see my local priest, Father Paul, sitting there. Confused, not sure what was happening, I slowly remembered the day I became on fire. "My children? How are they?" The priest looked at me, judging what to say, his eyes seeming to balance the situation.

"Your second son, Armand-Claude, has died. He received the last rites and has been buried in the family cemetery." Gently, he paused. "But the others live."

I felt suddenly as if my own soul was ready to leap after Armand-Claude to be with him. Inside a dreadful void, a horrible sadness filled me, and I saw I was going to live, even if I did not want to. One of my children, lost and dead.

"The other children wish to see you, Madame, if you are up to it, but you must be aware—they will look different now."

Not quite comprehending, I nodded yes, of course I would like to see my children.

My son and daughter walked slowly into the room, still weak after the struggle with smallpox. I could not breathe. No more the beautiful, carefree children, but their faces now weak and scarred by pox marks, ravaged by the disease. Beautiful smiles grew on their faces, as they saw me, their Mama. The smiles caused furrows of scars to become deeper, for now they were marred with the marks of near-death. However a beautiful, entrancing love enveloped them and my tears changed to ones of joy.

Then quietly I asked the priest, "May I have a mirror?" He answered softly, "Are you ready for this, Madame?" I answered, "Yes, I am"

He handed me a mirror and I saw the same ghastly marks all over my face. My physical beauty was gone forever, as was the beauty of my children. I said slowly, as if to understand all of this, "My sweet child has died. It says in the book of Job, The Lord gives, the Lord takes away. Blessed be the name of the Lord. I thank God for all my children." And I hugged them, and they fell in relief into my arms, and their hair smelled so good and full of life, and their little giggles warmed me. But in the year of our Lord,

1672, Armaud-Claude lay in a coffin in the cold and dark ground, and I shrieked inside. And soon in the same year, another child joined him in the cemetery.

I felt sad always and I listened in the early morning before I woke up for his sweet voice, and he was never there: where was the sound of my small son's running steps, his welcome smile and happy eyes!

Like the author of the Psalms, in distress I cried out,

Have mercy on me, Lord, because I am weak:
Lord, heal me.
Every moment diminishes my being:
You alone can heal me, O my celestial Love.

Jacques too became gaunt, and I felt surrounded by need so deep I could not begin to help. One afternoon Jacques came home with an ashen complexion.

"Go to bed, dear, and say your prayers," was all I could say.

He looked sharply at me, his throat convulsively jerking, and soon I heard his tired feet walking slowly up the stairs. I followed and placed my hand on his forehand but found no fever. I pulled a chair up to his bed and placed two bowls of soup on a small table next to him.

Then he commanded, "Take those bowls away or I will throw them out of the window."

Tense and shaking, I wanted to yell back; but instead, a small inner feeling told me to be quiet. I walked over to the window and looked at the courtyard below and saw a strong peasant who works for us walking up to our house carrying fresh bread. A healthy and happy brown dog frisked at his heels.

Suddenly for the first time in months, I laughed. "Toss it, dear. Break it! What a life we have: sad and sorrowful. I dare you to. I would love to hear the crash of the china. Life isn't meant to be like this. Here–I get the first throw!"

Aghast, Jacques stared at me and then his lips turned slightly up.

Impulsively, I turned towards him. "I want to live, Jacques, and live deeply, but I don't know how. Armand-Claude is gone and is with Christ. I know that beyond all else; I know our child is with Christ forever. But we are still here and what do we do? Mourn forever? Carry our bodies around like they are already carcasses? No, Christ lives in us. Let us praise God for caring for our dear son. Then let us let divine love transform our lives." And then in a quiet moment, we looked at each other, and I knew that somehow the truth of Christ had slipped out of me unexpectedly

Jacques said, "Jeanne, let us travel around the River Loire and spend time together. Could we be husband and wife after all of this sorrow? And I, so much older than you, can you bear this? Will you come away with me?"

I reached over and took his hand. "Yes, Jacques. I will go with you! I love the rivers and no one knows them like you. Will you teach me the currents and the twists and the beauty of the rivers of France? But first, shall we eat the soup?"

Jacques and Jeanne retreated together, finding some renewed sense of peace. And their next child was named Jean-Baptiste.

Spiritual Growth

I was never the same. Somehow in the horror after the deaths of my two children, I found an inner strength, a clear joy, a power, all clustered around my faith that my son now lived with Christ. I went deep inside and came up with a profound respect for life. My spiritual, interior life flourished.

I called this new spiritual growth annihilation: our natural life destroyed and in its place, the believer now knew the real power of the Spirit. I no longer feared what would happen. I knew that Christ had genuinely delivered me from evil. I now lived what Paul had written, "I no longer live, but Christ lives in me." (Galatians 2:20)

I did not look upon my losses as suffering caused by fate, but the loving blows of Christ, who wanted only the best for me. With this faith, I became a renewed person, born into Christ and the Spirit.

A servant stared at me standing in my closet, quickly grabbing for my dress.

"I want my blue dress. That neckline is too low." I look at the revealing, golden-laced gown the servant offered me and I remembered walking heavily, nothing spontaneous allowed, because of the restriction in that decorated gown.

The servant complained. "This one, Madame, is most becoming. The blue one, wear that one to church." The servant dismissed the blue dress with a wave of her arm.

I walked toward my dressing room. Once there, searching for the familiar blue color, the color of dancing rivers, I felt the familiar warmth of the Spirit again. Finding the comfortable gown, I quickly dashed into it. Then I ran out of the room, ignoring the servant's pleading, "Madame, the golden one..."

The Lord showed me to recommit myself to Him. My spiritual director, Mother Genevieve Granger, Prioress of the Benedictines, told me to take a vow to Jesus on July 22, 1672, on the day the church honors Mary Magdalene. She said to find a ring, go into my prayer closet and commit myself to Christ. I did as she suggested, knowing I wanted a solid relationship with Jesus Christ that would anchor me in His love. I put on my ring and said, "I vow pure love to God. I will obey God and whatever I believe to be his will. I will honor Jesus Christ." The solid-rock presence of Jesus Christ supported me and I knew that whatever happened, my life belonged to him.

I was tested quickly following these vows and could see more afflictions heading our way.

Jacques dismissed the carriage, entered the mansion, and started pacing around with his coat still on. I heard his heavy footsteps and ran to his side, yet he did not greet me.

"Husband," I started, but I stopped when I saw his glassy

eyes, strangely not comprehending. In a louder voice, I said loudly, "Jacques." Then I took his hand and turned him toward me. "What has happened?" I asked with a calm authority. He stared at me as if he did not know who I was. I took his coat off, sat him on a chair, and rubbed his hands between mine.

Jacques said in a low voice, "I am being sued. We may lose everything. And the king is already taxing most of our revenues." Then Jacques shouted, "And who is doing this, Jeanne? Do you know?"

I quietly shook my head no. "Your brother Father de la Mothe has schemed with the king's brother. It is a lie! They say we owe them 200,000 livres."

I was not surprised and sighed, resigned to this. "There are many discontented people out there, Jacques. My brother is one of them. They run to make trouble to relieve their distress. God will show us a way out of this."

The next morning Jacques lay in bed and I walked in peacefully after my morning prayers. "How do you feel now?"

"My gout has flared again. Everything hurts."

I began, "Jacques, I want to say something. I am gifted intellectually. . ."

"Yes. I have not liked that about you."

"Why not let me study the law and argue this case for you? Maybe this is God's reason I was sent to you: to protect your fortune for the well-being of our children."

Jacques felt increasingly nauseated. A woman studying the law? Ridiculous. And people already laughed at his strange wife who read the Bible and ministered to others. But suddenly he remembered the pale and vicious face of the opposing lawyer who talked to him yesterday.

Jacques turned to his wife, this strangely intelligent woman. Who but Jeanne could win this? His lips turned up slightly. "Would you help me, Jeanne?"

"Jacques, I am your wife; I am part of you." I rang the bell. "I will start researching the law today. Our God is a God of justice."

Jacques stared out the window onto the French pastoral countryside after she left. He saw Jeanne, in her usual modest attire, quickly walking to the carriage. And for the first time, he smiled. That opposing lawyer would not have a chance to win this, he reflected.

I prayed in the carriage and felt the impulse: not to the library; go straight to the judge. Peacefully I headed towards the court.

The law drew my attention—so influenced by divine justice—and following my father's advice, I spent hours studying in the legal libraries for an entire year. Through the law, I saw a different vision emerging—a vision of human rights. I understood detailed financial laws and wrote a legal document that destroyed the forces attacking my husband and me.

What happened next delighted me: many people came to me and asked for legal help. The Spirit opened the laws to me and won all these legal cases. With their new-found justice, they found a taste of the heavenly kingdom.

In the middle of my struggles, I became pregnant and gave birth to a healthy girl, my fifth child. With my humility, I thought of her as a sister and companion in life. I looked down at my sleeping infant daughter, glowing with warmth and health, and pondered the mystery of this child. I vowed, "I will raise this child as a child of joy. We will play, enjoy and serve God together. And, I pray, as I grow old we will know love as deep and intimate as the ocean of God."

Even with the birth of a new child, I continued my ministry. When she was a baby, I stayed up late at night, experimenting with herbs and making medicines. I understood skin problems and knew the suffering they caused. My medicines would mediate comfort, hope, and consolation.

Four months after the birth of Anne-Marie, another difficulty surfaced in my life. My older husband had grown increasingly ill and now lay weakly on his bed. I prepared for a final conversation with him, and as I did so, I remembered the sad wedding ceremony, my constant tears, the desire to die, yet all followed by the extraordinary gift of Christ within my heart. Now I prepared for my husband's approaching death.

Hearing the resounding bells of our parish church ringing, I walked to the large bed in which he lay. "My husband," I began, but he motioned for me to listen.

"I never deserved you, Jeanne," he said quietly. "I know I have put you through suffering and haven't cared for you well. I am sorry," and he grew quiet as tears started coursing from his eyes.

I could only answer truthfully. "We all grieve for our shortcomings. Jacques, look at our children. We learned to care," I said. "God is with you, listening to you and loving you. You will ascend to Christ at the right time." He nodded, and closed his eyes, exhausted from the effort of speaking.

And I, though everyone secretly said how fortunate that the sad marriage was over, knew grief as I looked at my dead husband. Alone, I wondered, "What will happen now? Human life seems like nothing. Nothing but Jesus Christ within me matters.

III
Spiritual Adventures

My daughter never knew her father, but I cared for her with divine assurance. As a widow with a huge estate, I saw the vultures gathering—my half-brother, a few bishops, some unmarried men who suggested that we marry. Why, as a woman I couldn't even legally own property! And now alone with a fortune, what would I do?

The Spirit warned me about these men showing up, one after another, asking for control of my money: their smiles, their offers of relieving me of what they called the burden of my estate.

My little Anne-Marie came running to me after they left to exclaim, "Mama! Be careful!" And I hugged her and sang a lullaby. And then I said, "Anne Marie, I see them. Quiet yourself. God is now my husband."

I studied the law again, consulted with friends of my father, and put all of the money in trusts for my children, with a small allowance for us. Then when they pleaded for control of my money, I gently explained that this problem was solved and the news of my solid trusts brought frowns to their faces.

"God has provided for us, Anne-Marie," I would confidently whisper in her ears.

A child's voice filled the room. "Mama," Anne-Marie said lazily. "What are we going to do today?"

"Today," I explained, "we will visit the sick and take my ointments that I have made for their wounds."

"Mama," the child continued. "I like to see them get well."

"So do I, daughter."

We hugged before gathering our medical equipment together.

I had created serious opposition by my protection of my wealth, and once again my half-brother, Father de la Mothe, began pondering how to improve his life. I could see this situation from his perspective and knew that he was still planning more attacks.

Father de la Mothe had looked at his dead brother-in-law Jacques Guyon lying in the coffin, in the immense room surrounded by fine French furniture, wine racks on the wall.

Even with all this wealth, his sister Jeanne stood there in a plain blue dress, devoid of jewelry. With all these resources, why didn't his simpleton sister even try to look elegant? Her eldest son, lines between his eyes, stood there watching his mother. Yet, Father de la Mothe admitted to himself, many people respected his sister and many aristocratic French families had travelled great distances to the funeral.

Shaking his head, he looked at his simple room at the Barnabite monastery and thought again of the large mansion reserved for the head of his order, and the visiting Vatican dignitaries that frequented that palace. The distance between his room and that palace presented itself as desirable yet impassable.

Hitting his fist against the table, he fumed: his rich sister, Jeanne, why did she have all the wealth? And he, his gifts never recognized, left as an obscure Barnabite brother. Did he really want this life? His life was passing quickly and nothing would ever happen unless he took the initiative. He wanted that mansion.

Taking off his interior gloves, he made his plan. "That witch won the law suit," he thought. "There must be another way to get her estate and influence." What is her Achilles heel? Why, that is an easy question! Always her spirituality—she takes that direction too seriously.

How do I use this? Why had this never occurred to me before, he wondered, his thoughts racing. Get her a spiritual director she will enjoy and then find a way to control the director. Jeanne will be obedient. My order and I will get her money. My religious order will reward me for gaining this fortune for them, and Jeanne will be reduced to a submissive, docile woman.

And so the plan was conceived that would carry me closer to the heart of Jesus Christ.

Father de la Mothe sent me a letter of introduction to Father François La Combe, a well-known Barnabite brother. Father La Combe experienced the adulation of many as an eloquent spiritual director. Receiving the letter, I agreed to this spiritual direction, because I needed a new spiritual director.

I kept telling everyone, this interior way of relating to Christ changes everything in our lives. Prayer, I said, was like jumping into a roaring river and letting the rapids carry us to wherever God wills. And the roaring river of God found me and began to carry me to different places.

The good Father La Combe approached my home with care: I was sure he had heard many warnings about my persuasive qualities from my half-brother. When he first saw me, I could see he liked me, even though his eyes briefly glanced at my small-pox scars.

I began by talking of the scriptures. "I want to know more about what God is revealing through the Bible—I have read this for so many years—and I want to know what I should do. My husband is dead now and I do not wish to marry again, for many reasons."

The priest nodded as he began to take in my ideas.

I continued, "And as you know, the bishops of our church want me to donate my money to their causes, yet I see this as a resource for my children; so I have put it in trusts."

"I see." Father La Combe did understand. All church groups wanted lots of money.

After talking of spiritual inspiration, La Combe said openly, "I do want you to understand that I might be moving to Geneva soon, but let's continue to talk."

In ensuing weeks, I talked to him again and again and began to see that he loved the Lord with tenderness and devotion. Under his influence, I began to grow and expand spiritually.

Father La Combe began to tell me of his new ideas. One day he sat in his chair, eyes closed, praying. As my spiritual director, he felt an unusual instinct. What was this thought presenting itself so powerfully in his mind?

"Tell Madame Guyon to write." The words sprang into his consciousness.

What? Tell a woman to write? That must not be done, he reiterated. Hadn't he always heard that women didn't write and think? They were followers, more like animals needing guidance. Again his conscience spoke. "Didn't she minister to you? Why limit her to only talking? If she writes, many will be blessed be her words." Father La Combe decided, I will tell her tomorrow. If the Spirit wished to change this message, I would accept that. Otherwise, I will speak these unusual words to her.

The next day, Father La Combe came to visit me. "The Spirit has given me a message for you."

I waited expectantly.

Father La Combe looked at his lap and spoke softly. "You are to write about God. You are to write frequently. And you will have many spiritual children out of your writings."

I walked over to look out of the window. "I have thought this many times myself, Father. But what will I say? I have no idea of what to write."

Father La Combe stood up, breathing out deeply. "That is up to the Spirit."

Without turning to see, I heard him closing the door.

I then slowly walked to my desk. Picking up paper, I sensed a rush of images of suffering men and women. "Teach them to pray. Tell them about my passionate love."

My words flooded out, sparkling with powerful light.

One day Father La Combe spoke out. "At times, I feel like you should be the director, not I, as I am not sure if I will have any legacy. I see that you write well. Continue writing!"

With these words, I felt like a net that threatened to entangle me was cut open, and like a bird I flew away free. If I wrote, I thought, I would continue to know the will of God. If I became part of the frantic world, I might lose my soul forever.

Quickly I wanted to affirm La Combe and his ministry. "I have heard you preach, Father. I hear your intensity for the living God."

I stood up quickly, facing him directly. "You will leave behind the living, forceful Word of God, the truth spoken from the Holy Spirit."

He froze and then quietly moved toward the door. Our time together for that day was finished, yet somehow we knew our very real spiritual connection would last forever.

Father La Combe glanced back to see me sitting in my chair, as I prayed intently for him.

In the days to come, the Lord spoke to him and called him to a new ministry in Geneva. In faith he responded and moved quickly to this city, a place where the Catholic Church had an active outreach ministry.

My prayer led me into direct service to human need. With Anne-Marie trailing close behind, I walked into an elderly peasant woman's hut. The woman's bloodshot eyes met my direct gaze.

"What is wrong, Genevieve?"

"It is too shameful."

"Nothing is shameful before our merciful Lord. Jesus knows all of our agonies."

Genevieve looked away quietly. Then quickly, before she could change her mind, she pulled up her bedclothes. Bed sores covered her buttocks and in the open wounds, white maggots squirmed.

Genevieve covered her face, crying quietly.

I turned and whispered to Anne-Marie. "Go quickly, Little One. Bring me the green jar of ointment."

"Mama," Anne-Marie whispered, "You aren't going to touch those, are you?"

"Child, God is with us. We offer healing in God's name."

Anne-Marie turned, running away. She fumbled in my bag, found the jar, and slowly walked into the small cottage.

I reached out, gently touching Anne-Marie's hair and then turned to Genevieve and took her hand. "Holy Spirit, be among us, healing and restoring in the name of Jesus."

Quickly I leaned over, rubbing my home-made medicine into each wound. Genevieve sighed with relief, exhaling out weariness and suffering.

"The maggots are gone, Madame. Have Claude wash the bed linens. And please send him to get me if you need me again."

Anne-Marie and I walked quietly out to the waiting carriage.

"Mama, why didn't they call the doctor?"

"No doctor will visit these poor villages, Anne-Marie. But God has shown me how to make medicine, and I study late at night to know what herbs to use. I hope to start a hospital for the poor. But until then, Anne-Marie, we will help with my ointments." I turned towards the young child and said with joyful confidence. "My homemade medicines get better and better."

Anne-Marie climbed into the carriage with me. I instructed the driver where the next hut was that we would visit.

Now I saw some small changes in my mother-in-law Therese.

"Therese, how many do we have ready?" The aroma of baking bread filled the house.

Therese crept towards the dining room, her hands crippled and worn. She counted the loaves of waiting bread.

"Jeanne, we have nearly two hundred loaves ready."

Moving into the room rapidly, I nearly stepped on Anne-Marie who sat on the floor building towers of wooden blocks.

I paused. "Let's aim for three hundred loaves for Friday."

Looking at Therese, I prayed for release from the memories of the dreadful tensions between us: Christ within asked this of me.

Therese paused in the face of this beauty—the poor being fed, the happy grandchild playing, and the powerful presence.

I continued, "I am going out to the village and find poor children to help in this food give-away. I will pay them a decent wage."

Therese said quietly, "And I will pay their first week's wages."

During my times of prayer, I sensed a new call from the Lord.

Leave your home and go.
But go where?
To Geneva.
Geneva? Where so many Protestants live? Would they learn from me or I from them?

There had always been the River in my childhood, flowing to worlds unknown. The mysterious River brought kings and adventure and wonders.

At sunrise, the lapping of the River Loire quietly greeted my daughter and me, along with two devoted servants as we walked toward the boat. Every step I took made me stronger. I looked back to see if they were going to pursue us and stop us from leaving, for I had kept my plans secret so that the authorities would not stop us.

Walking down to the swift-flowing river, Anne-Marie stumbled sleepily. "Where are we going, Mama?"

"Away, Anne-Marie, on a long journey. We are going to Geneva, where Father La Combe also ministers. We will travel on the river and go to Melun where we will travel in a stagecoach. An adventure on the river will be fun—we will see so much on this journey—but we must be very quiet for the first few hours."

As we hiked, images flooded my mind. I remembered the first welcome cry of Armand-Claude, now dead in the family cemetery; my husband Jacques and our conflicted home together; the hungry, poor peasants suffering everywhere.

And now—the flame-red passion of God. "I am who I am" reverberated through my mind.

"I am the good shepherd."
"I am the Way, the Truth, the Life."
The ecstasy of I Am touched me, joined with me.

Anne-Marie gasped. "Mama, it is beautiful here." The yellow sunlight glittered on the blue river, birds chirping, the peaceful river praising the new day through its dancing eddies and twirls.

"Mama, why do we love Christ so much?"

"Christ is within us, Anne-Marie. He knows our hearts, sorrows, and struggles. Now off we go! We go to love and adventure. To Christ we entrust ourselves."

I firmly grabbed the boat, lifted Anne-Marie in, and we floated away, abandoning ourselves to a divine journey. Our boat glided smoothly off to a new life in Geneva.

IV
Geneva

I thought of it as abandoning myself to Christ: to trust Christ in even the smallest details of life. And my faith carried us on this journey to our new home. Lake Geneva looked pure and clean with its blues and greens, reminding me of the colors of life. Blue water next to the green plants tells us of the Lord's sustenance and nourishment. Soon the gentle push of new life began.

I went to introduce myself to the Bishop of Geneva. After many conversations with him, Anne-Marie and I settled outside of Geneva at a place called Gex, surrounded by the high and lofty Jura mountain range peaks. At the beginning, I lived in a convent for new Catholics and supported them with my finances. Father La Combe had become an acclaimed preacher in Geneva and when he had time, a group of us prayed with him. Soon a vision for helping the poor sick came to us, and I worked nonstop to organize and build hospitals staffed by volunteers.

Many church leaders, including the Bishop of Geneva, begged me to become a nun and lead a convent and donate my fortune to the church. I refused. I had found something better: the glorious free life of the Spirit.

One day a group of us traveled on a pass through the tall mountains to a small town, Thonon. Craggy and pointed, the mountain peaks seemed to point to the eternal skies. Huge grey rocks, hard and forbidding, provided a presence of strength and permanence. And looking at my friends, I gave thanks for such a moment.

I picked up Anne-Marie and hugged her. "We have started a hospital, Anne-Marie! Today it opened. Father La Combe and a group of us from Gex worked together and found donated rooms. Someone gave us twelve beds. Three people have donated themselves to serving in this hospital without pay. Already it is filled with the sick, and soon we hope to expand this hospital to include those poor widows who have nowhere to turn for support."

Anne-Marie threw her arms around my neck.

I nearly danced with happiness. "Anne-Marie, the nurses use my ointments and medicines. God has fulfilled my dream of helping the sick who have no doctors!"

I met whenever I could with Father La Combe in Geneva.

"Father, how your ministry has prospered! I hear about your sermons and spiritual direction. Your inward peace ministers and reaches out to many."

The good priest smiled at me.

"And you, my dear? Your hospital has done well and I hear now another one is starting. God is using your medicines to heal."

I tried to express my happiness. "There is no satisfaction like the joy of abandonment to Christ. Now I am called to serve others who are seeking God. I ask your prayers for Anne-Marie and me as we start on new travels to help others."

La Combe responded, "I may see you, your lovely daughter, and 'Family,' as I continue on my preaching schedule." I laughed at his use of the nickname Family for the woman who served as my servant. Now she was our Family and we called her that name.

We prayed together and I left his office, oddly aware, though, of the stares of an unknown man watching me from a side street.

Late one night I wrote about the connections between souls. "Recently in the light of God I have seen the origin and nature of spiritual unions. We depend on each other and become united to one another. When through the light of God we understand this, our journey of faith is beautiful!

"The human being, created in the image of God, personally experiences restoration from the Fall by the means of our indwelling Lord. Because of Christ within, the believer partakes of the divine nature of God. After receiving the divine nature, the believer becomes fertile and communicates grace to others. Through this union with God, Christians touch other believers and they mutually share grace."

I received pleas for help from many. Some nuns came to me telling me of priests pushing for sexual behavior with them. I confronted the bishop about priests under his spiritual authority. I remember the tense scene in Geneva with the Bishop D'Aranthon. "Bishop, your assistant is out of line. Once again, he is seeking a girlfriend from your nuns."

The bishop, dressed in black and purple, sighed. Standing up, he announced, "I will address this myself." And I knew he would, for Christ within assured me that this was accomplished.

I felt the growing tension. The more I ministered, the more fulfilled I became, but I also felt the growing displeasure from others, such as the Bishop of Geneva. I was told to stop by many afraid of the rising political tensions. And

I couldn't. I loved the presence of the Spirit too much to stop.

Even with this, life, joyful life, continued between my daughter and me. We traveled around Geneva where peak after peak of white, snow-covered mountain ranges surrounded us, a circle of the mysterious wonders of the earth.

I strapped on Anne-Marie's home-made skates. "Hold onto my hands." I quickly walked on the frozen Alpine pond. Anne-Marie faced me directly, clinging to both of my hands. I kept our balance while Anne-Marie slid, fell, and gasped. Laughing, I encouraged her, "Use me as your balance! Hold on, Anne-Marie!" Little by little, Anne-Marie slid her skates in harmony with me. Then, floating, Anne-Marie and I, centered and glowing, skated over the pond together. Dazzled by the white, mysterious Alps sheltering the two tiny skaters, we glided over the ice in pure harmony.

In March 1685, I wrote in *A Short and Easy Method of Prayer*, "All are called to this joy of God, in this life and in the one to come. I say, all people are called to essential blessedness, and likewise all are called to the enjoyment of God. God alone is happiness. I say the enjoyment of God, and not only of the gifts of God, for the gifts alone would not satisfy because they would not content the believer. Our own spirit is so noble that even the most exalted gifts of God cannot make us happy unless God Himself is given with the gifts. God's whole desire is to give the divine being to us."

The young nun whom I helped escape from the sexual advances of the bishop's assistant came to my house one day. "Madame, I must ask you to please protect yourself more. I know people are trying to destroy you. I couldn't sleep all last night." She and I both knew that the legal system could still burn people at the stake.

Sighing, I slowly walked to the window and looked at the green open fields rolling down to the beaches on the magnificent lake.

"How many will be killed by the Inquisition?" the young nun sorrowfully asked.

I turned toward her, "I understand the dangers of my writing, but the thoughts come from Christ. I will continue to write them and trust in whatever God wills."

The young nun started crying. I walked over to her, "Little one, you will learn that life is all about having the courage to live in God's justice. Don't cry for me. I understand that the great purpose of Christ surrounds my life. I rest on Him."

Anne-Marie knew not about the concerns I harbored. I woke up in the middle of the night, contemplating, wondering. I sensed people in spiritual agony. The peasants were dying of famine, while Louis and the nobility created a luxurious society at Versailles. Yet, here in this small town near Geneva, alone with my young child, I knew personal contentment and began to write about my own experiences in hopes that through this, others will know Christ as I do.

Soon a government official from Parliament visited me.

"I hear that you are writing about prayer," he started simply. "I too want to know how to pray."

I stood and looked at him. The moment was here: Was that the distant ringing of the bell? My destiny had taken a step closer.

"Yes."

"I wish to read what you have written. It is clear to me, Madame, that you understand more than you say."

I understood that this man would begin publishing my books. I quietly picked up my handwritten manuscript and handed it to this powerful man.

Soon the book was published everywhere! First a small number of books appeared. Then requests started growing, and now a second edition. People from all over Europe wished to read my words teaching all how to find Christ within.

Four editions, five editions, six editions ... And where would these books take me?

Watch and wait.

Yet the Bishop of Geneva became mistrusting of me, and he ordered me to leave his diocese. I trusted Christ to lead us, and soon homes were open to me all over Europe as women asked me to live with them and help with their spiritual development.

My daughter and I traveled so many places. Let me try to remember all of the places. Geneva, Gex, Thonon, Turin, Grenoble, Marseilles, Nice, Genoa, and Vercelli. What a set of adventures! I saw the world and the beauties of natural creation. How many women can say that? We traveled, learned, suffered, laughed, and lived deeply, very deeply.

But it was more than that, for now I sensed my spirit within me. I was not a forlorn widow, but a joyful, laughing woman. I left behind pettiness, brushed off greed, and knew spiritual contentment.

I knew life was screeching, unsatisfied desire for most of the nobles at Versailles, but Anne-Marie and I lived a different life. We lived simply, ate what the locals ate, and lived wonderfully. We saw the Swiss Alps covered with snow and traveled on horseback through dense mountain passes. We smelled rich, pure mountain air. One day I watched Anne-Marie run across the mountain fields, laughing with delight at the sheer freedom of our life. And I sat on a tree stump, delighting in the beauty of nature, praying to my interior Christ who was giving us this experience of beauty.

And I, Jeanne Guyon, understood that historical movements and actions would enter my life, turning it upside down, and soon I would take a place on the world stage. King Louis XIV, the Sun King, and his whole court of Versailles, Archbishop Fénelon and Bishop Bossuet had become aware of my writing (hard to believe!) and soon the thoughts and actions of their hearts and minds would impact my future. But I knew that God's eternal decrees were to be trusted, and I rested on this truth.

V
At Versailles
The Sun King

I knew that Christ asked me to treasure his Word shown in the scriptures and love the wisdom He gave me. When we love Christ, we become a new and transformed person, and this was all I desired. Yet, living in the mid-to late 1600s in France, at the time of the powerful King Louis XIV, I heard the conflicted clash between different visions for humanity ringing louder and louder. I believed in the vision of human dignity and freedom based in the redemption of Christ. At Versailles, Louis advocated a vision of human glory based on military victories and, of course, physical pleasures. In my lifetime, the spiritual conflict between the different beliefs would grow into huge social conflicts. Indeed, after Christ became involved with my life, Louis' whole court at Versailles was turned upside-down.

I thought of my own life from the human perspective as nothing, but because I walked in the presence of Christ, I had something to say. Jesus Christ has looked upon us and loved us, and because of that, each one of us is important. If we surrender our lives to Christ, we know the eternal glory of God in our lives.

Others did not agree with me. King Louis wanted his court to be recognized as a place of exquisite beauty. But even he could not control the fact that his life was seen by others. We all remembered his constantly-changing lovers, the gambling parties, and the heavy taxes. But I, Jeanne Guyon, witnessed another side of Versailles and I wrote it down. I saw a moment of living holiness in noble leaders, in heads of government trying to seek God. This was exciting to me. I had loyal friends in Louis' court, and their presence delighted me.

I feared that the history of this famous court would disappear. I knew that God in his goodness taught us that history must be remembered or humanity would never learn. And somehow, I sensed someone, I knew not who, was writing the history for Versailles just as fast as Louis lived it.

You know, we writers recognize one another. We who record details and the broad stuff of history, who record our thoughts, feelings and emotions, sense others doing the same. So I was not concerned, even though I knew not who it was.

Now I will add the part of the history I learned from the good Duc de Saint-Simon, who carefully and sacrificially wrote this history down. In his memoirs, he captured all the experiences that Louis wanted forgotten. This duke detailed everything, writing away in his study, locking up all his papers, and telling no one about his historical work. In living through this era of history, I saw how Christ's actions changed all of our lives in the court of King Louis XIV.

At Versailles

Both this historian and the entire court at Versailles watched Louis' personal life. While married to someone else, he had a girlfriend named Madame de Montespan, but called Athénaïs. Together this couple planned revelries, plays and parties at Versailles. Always beautifully dressed, Athénaïs seemed to delight in her public life as Louis' paramour. Many children were born to this unlikely couple. Athénaïs gave the children after they were born to a nanny, Madame de Maintenon, who cared for them.

Athénaïs felt like her entire security was based on this relationship with the king. At times she feared he would leave her, so she began the practice of seeking out a woman, Catherine Deshayes Voisin, who made love potions. Athénaïs would slip these secret chemicals into Louis' drinks.

Rumors of what Athénaïs and Catherine were doing reached Louis' ears.

"Arrest that witch Catherine," he ordered. But quietly Louis sent a message to his Chief of Police La Reynie to keep all the records only for the king's eyes. Catherine was to be taken to the fortressed prison at the Vincennes with its huge ominous towers. The tower called The Keep announced to all those unfortunate enough to see it that their life could be obliterated by the power of the Sun King.

And the powerful Gabriel Nicolas de La Reynie, Lieutenant-General of Police in France, publicly brought Catherine in for interrogation, as they called it. At the Vincennes they tortured Catherine, and after her forced confession, the French authorities ordered that Catherine Deshayes Voisin be burned alive in 1680. This was done. The Affair of the Poisons, they called this scandal at Versailles.

Even after this, their relationship continued. Athénaïs talked about everything with Louis except the fate of poor Catherine. "How is everything, Sire? I hear all of the compliments about your courageous declaration of Versailles as the official seat of the French government. I am pleased not to have to travel to Paris now," Athénaïs started.

Louis flushed. "Have you heard what that troublesome Bishop Bossuet said? He called Versailles the City of the Rich. This religious man said that Versailles needed no enemies because this place carries its own seeds of destruction."

Louis declared, "I am deciding what to do about this now. How are our children?"

"They are with the nanny. She does such a good job with them."

"Wait until I visit the nursery. Then we will have time together."

Louis strode down the hall and turned the corner to see the nanny, Madame de Maintenon, cradling his latest daughter. Louis watched this woman, devoid of jewelry and pretense, kissing his children.

"Madame," he began. His nanny jumped up. "Sire, what an honor this is!"

"Sit, please. I have come to see the Duc de Maine."

The crippled duke, Louis Auguste, struggled over, and greeted his father warmly. In concern, Madame de Maintenon hovered over and around the boy.

"How is your leg doing?" Louis inquired.

Louis Auguste swayed, his crutches unstable. Madame de Maintenon helped him balance and said, "We have not found a doctor that can help, but I still search for assistance."

"Madame, tell me more about yourself."

"Sire, that is difficult to do. I have had a tempestuous life."

"Continue."

"My father died when I was two. We were French Protestants living on the island of Martinique. My mother struggled to keep our family fed, and frequently we wondered if we would survive, even after we returned to France." Taking a breath, she continued. "Soon after, I became a Catholic. As a teenager I married Paul Scarron."

Louis frowned. "That older, crippled poet?"

"Yes, Sire. He died several years ago. When Paul died, I too wanted to die. I was alone." She started talking rapidly. "Thank you, Sire, for offering me this position as your royal nanny."

Louis reached down to caress Louis Auguste's cheek. He had left without a good-bye to Athénaïs who paled at his quick departure. Louis continued his solitary journey down the long corridors of Versailles. Everywhere people bowed and curtseyed without once drawing his attention.

The next day Louis entered the nursery energetically. "Tonight, Madame de Maintenon, may we have dinner?"

Madame de Maintenon paused. Then with deliberation, she spoke, "I am no mistress, Sire. I will be your wife or nothing to you. I say that respectfully—no matter what you decide, I will still care for your wonderful children."

Louis loved these children from his mistresses more than those from his wives. Somehow Madame de Maintenon's love for these children touched Louis' heart and he chose her as his wife.

In January 1684, the archbishop of Paris Harlay watched as Madame de Maintenon walked down the aisle in the Royal Chapel at Versailles in the dazzling glow of candlelight shining on the gold-plated décor. The attractive older woman smiled at the glowing King Louis who waited for her. The Archbishop shivered and started the ancient rite of Holy Matrimony as they took vows one to another, witnessed only by the archbishop, the King's confessor, Father de la Chaise, and his body servant, Bontemps.

"We will not let my subjects know of this marriage," Louis informed the Archbishop of Paris. "I have told Madame de Maintenon that this morganatic marriage would not be accepted in France. I am expected to be with a beauty, such as Madame de Montespan."

The archbishop, his eyes lowered, waited.

"Madame de Maintenon is a woman I can trust."

The archbishop blinked a couple of times. Only time will tell how the enigmatic Madame de Maintenon will roil the entire court at Versailles.

According to the court historian Duc de Saint-Simon, Madame de Maintenon influenced Louis and encouraged him to see the world the way she did. A former Protestant herself, she detested Protestants as those full of spiritual disease and contaminating all of French society.

Soon the victim in France was the peaceful law, the Edict of Nantes. Louis XIV revoked the Edict of Nantes in 1685 and all Protestants were outlawed. This edict had allowed Protestants to live in peace in Catholic France.

From Louis XIV's legal document proceeded the powerful words. "We forbid our subjects of the religion called Reformed to meet any more for the exercise of the said religion in any place or private house under any pretext whatever."

I, Jeanne Guyon, saw the end of safety for our French Protestants: no meetings, no schools; to be Protestant was outlawed. The sounds of screaming Protestants echoed through the land as they were dragged from their homes and some murdered. Fortunately, many successfully fled from their homeland.

With the end of Protestants in France, everything began to be turned upside-side down. Who knew what would happen next? And then the church attacked, using its desolate power against me. My popular books encouraged an interior life lived with Christ. The church authorities heard this as a challenge to their power, and some thought of me as heretical. The Roman Catholic bishop of Geneva judged me harshly. On November 4, 1687, a pastoral letter of Bishop of Geneva, Jean d'Aranthon, condemned my famous book, *A Short and Easy Method of Prayer.*

The Revocation of the Edict of Nantes awakened some to the spiritual need of France. A famous Archbishop Francois

Fénelon answered the call to try to help his conflicted country. Fénelon taught the Duke of Burgundy, grandson of Louis, and trained him to be a wise and just ruler.

Father Fénelon walked into the royal classroom. He saw the waiting Duke of Burgundy, the heir to Louis' throne, and met his eyes with a steady gaze.

"Now a lesson, my future king. How will you judge the character of those who help you rule this great kingdom of France? You will need trusted and loyal advisors who will provide you with words of truth and love for your subjects. But how you will find them, and how will you know if they are fit to help you rule France?"

The duke stood up and said simply, "I will keep them close with me. They will live with me at Versailles. We will hunt together and I will observe them always, like my grandfather does."

"Observe what, little king? How they slaughter animals? So you will know that one day they can slaughter you?"

The duke paused. "I will give them tough problems to solve and test their understanding."

The archbishop continued to push. "You will know their intelligence then. But their character? How do you know who to trust? They will all want your attention, your power. You need trusted advisors who understand effective principles, yet are loyal to you."

The duke shrugged. "Of course they will be loyal to me. I will have all the power."

"No, do not dismiss this problem. I recommend a simple way to judge people's character, a way that the ancient Greeks used. Observe how people you are considering for positions treat their friends. Do they use friends to obtain higher positions and then desert them? If they do, these are people to be shunned. Or do they have a few chosen, trustworthy friends in whose company is intimacy and warmth? Look for men and women who strive for living holiness, who are with one another because of love, not for profit. The best test of a person's character is in their relationships with friends. In friendship there are no external constraints, no legal requirements, and no social pressures, as with other relationships. In a friendship loyalty and love may emerge, but a vexatious and greedy spirit may also be seen.

"Be careful, my future king. Use such a simple test and you will find those that will help you rule France with wisdom."

VI
My First Incarceration

Because of the popularity of my books, I knew I was in danger, but my contentment supported my life. I wrote many nights and cared for others during the day. How I wished this time in my life could last forever! But, that was not meant to be, and trouble fell upon me suddenly.

My half-brother Father de la Mothe still schemed for control of my money and estate. Then he turned the powers of the Inquisition on my spiritual director, Father La Combe.

They invited Father La Combe to Paris to preach, and after he arrived ultimatums were given to him: As my spiritual director he was to order me to stop writing and ministering. Or he, the good Father, would suffer the consequences.

Father La Combe said he could not deny the work of the Spirit in me. The Archbishop of Paris Harlay arranged that this gifted man be arrested and incarcerated. As of October 3, 1687, Father La Combe suffered imprisonment.

The strength of God had entered the soul of Father La Combe. He had written strong words about the spiritual life.

"If we aspire after Christian perfection, we must disengage ourselves and forego all that concerns our own interest, to have God alone in view. This is the generous charity; this is the purity of love. All self-interested motives are imperfect, because in them we seek ourselves. Walk in the most excellent way, which is that of disinterestedness."

And then, in January, 1688, the authorities arrested me and took me to an unventilated room in a Parisian convent without windows and locked me in. My Anne-Marie was eleven years old. I remembered my grief the day they arrested me and tore my Anne-Marie away from me.

I tried to express this in my poems.

I am nearly destroyed by the storm and the waves,
Falling down on me, I see this horrible tempest;
Lightning strikes on my head
Taking away my hope and all rest.

Come to my help, only Author of my flame,
Without you, I will perish:
Guide my troubled soul;
Alas! Come down to help me.

I was locked in a small room in the nunnery at the Convent of the Visitation. With no window, hot, stifling, I sat in a hard chair. Where was Anne-Marie? Who looked after her? Would she be abused or hurt?

I looked at my hands again and picked up the Bible. Quietly I turned to the book of Job to read of the one who suffered. After the death of his children, Job sat in the dirt, rubbing his open sores with broken pottery pieces, hoping to stop the oozing pain of the boils. "Curse God and die," his wife said to him.

And why not, I thought. What has my faith gotten me? A list of problems sprang to my mind: incarcerated, humiliated, tormented, separated from my children, where was Anne-Marie?

I stared at the hard, narrow bed on which I slept and sighed.

Yet they couldn't incarcerate the love of Christ. Worldly powers would like to if they could.

Christ's love sought me. Gently I felt again the warm Spirit reflecting on me, dazzling my senses, and I breathed deeply.

I still knew the operations and graces of God. I recognized the secret designs of God in my life. Woven deep into my soul were hopes and designs God had for me. Like fossils buried deep within the soil, the divine plan of Christ emerged: a ministry here, a personal revelation here, and a delight God had planned.

Remembering the serene ice skating in the Alps with Anne-Marie, I breathed out a deep inner prayer to my young daughter. "Hold on to my hands, Anne-Marie. Keep your balance." I knew that prayer from genuine human need reached God as quickly as lightening streaking across the sky. For a brief instant I saw in my mind Anne-Marie safely at home with one of my relatives, and I wept with relief, understanding the truth of my vision. Christ had not left me desolate and would sustain Anne-Marie.

The Archbishop of Paris Harlay visited me one day.
He sat close and talked in low tones.
"I know how to get your freedom."
I answered, "Please do!"

He paused. "I have a good plan. You will sign to have Anne-Marie marry my nephew, and I will sign a document to have you released."

Quickly, I stood and answered loudly. "Never will I sign this! She is eleven years old and not nearly old enough for marriage. And she does not know your nephew."

I knew that Harlay wanted my money for his nephew. My Anne-Marie would have no arranged marriage, even if this caused my incarceration to continue.

This conviction alone carried me through hours of interrogations conducted by Inquisition officials from my Roman Catholic Church. I protested my innocence and said that I was a faithful daughter of the church. My release, however, came not from my answers to their piercing questions, but from my spunky and loving cousin.

At Versailles, Madame de Maintenon conversed with Elise de la Maisonfort, my cousin. Elise wore the full black habit of her nunnery and taught at Maintenon's school at St. Cyr.

Later Elise told me the conversation.

"My cousin, a kind and loving woman, needs your help, Madame. She has been incarcerated in the Convent of the Visitation for almost a year now. We are not allowed to see her. Her half-brother started all of this because Jeanne refused to allow him control of her money after her husband died. Jeanne has steadfastly put her wealth in trusts for her children. Help us, I beg you." Elise stopped suddenly.

Madame de Maintenon paused. It was nearly time for her afternoon rendezvous with her husband, Louis XIV. Smoothing her hair, she said, "I will request that Louis have her released. If she is as you say, she can help us with my school at St. Cyr."

Sighing, Louis' wife wondered if this gold dress might enhance her own eye color. Or would another?

Then focusing on the impassioned nun, she gave her a gentle hug. Holding the nun at arm's length and looking directly into her eyes, she murmured, "Please pray for me. More and more I keep thinking that I want to die." Elise's eyes opened wide and with genuine warmth she responded, "Madame Guyon might be able to help. She has worked miracles helping the despair of many, because she found prayer helped her own unhappiness." Before leaving, Elise reached out and clasped the sad woman's hand.

Madame de Maintenon walked slowly to her own room. Praying as she fixed her hair, she went to put on a more elaborate dress. "Please, God, let not Louis' romantic interests go to another. What will happen to me if a mistress takes my place? I need to be queen for my security, and he has still not declared in public that I am even his wife." Maybe today she would allure Louis enough to make their marriage public; she still dreamed of being established as Queen of France.

She moved down the hall to the luxurious bedroom. She sat in the chair, momentarily catching her breath. Louis walked in. "My husband," she began before her words were silenced by their passion.

Within days, Madame de Maintenon arranged my release from incarceration. Now she invited me to exercise a privileged position as spiritual director at Versailles and St. Cyr.

In October, 1688, at Versailles, news buzzed of my now living among the royalty. Archbishop François Fénelon increasingly heard the name of Jeanne Guyon. He was told that six years earlier this freshly widowed woman had moved to Geneva to minister to others.

"Have you heard, Father Fénelon, what Madame Guyon did?" another priest questioned him one day.

Showing little interest, Fénelon waited. The priest continued, "They traveled all around Europe together. Father La Combe and this Guyon woman. And they had the audacity to deny that they were sleeping together."

Fénelon shrugged his shoulders. "Maybe they weren't. It is possible."

"But to make this worse, this Guyon wrote a book teaching people how to pray. How ridiculous to think that God would call a woman to be a theologian, or even for women to pray. So Louis incarcerated her for nearly a year."

Fénelon stood straighter and frowned. An extremely astute man, Louis had perceived something. He paused. "What happened in the incarceration?"

"This woman never admitted she had done anything wrong. Louis finally let her go because Madame de Maintenon felt sorry for her, but Father La Combe—they still have him incarcerated. And a good thing too—traveling with a woman and encouraging her to write. La Combe says she has God within her. What a scandal!"

Now with vague apprehension enveloping him, Fénelon gazed off into the distance. Then turning, he looked directly at the speaker and said quietly, "A most amazing story." What devotion, he thought. Journeying together, praying together, loving God together, they lived the Christian life in thought, word, and deed. Fénelon walked to his solitary dinner.

The next morning Father Fénelon watched the peasants toiling in green fields on the neighboring farm. "Bon jour, Abbe!" they greeted him. And slowly, ever so slowly, Fénelon strolled around, puzzling. At Versailles, the nobility frolicked, danced, ate, dressed elegantly, yet what did they lack?

Oblivious to the presence of this famous priest, a young man leaned over, caring for the flower garden. Fénelon felt his conviction rise. The peasants knew the power of God in the goodness of creation. Life here flowed clear in its essence with simplicity, love, wonder. But not at Versailles. Not in the intrigue at the City of the Rich, as Bossuet had called this place.

Fénelon waved at the young man, "Merci, merci."

Fénelon's questions continued to gather inner intensity and power. What force animated Madame Guyon? How could we have the vibrant life force of the peasants and still have our responsible positions in society? He tried to dismiss the questions; after all, he had a position at Versailles to maintain. Then the momentous day arrived.

Duchesse de Charost, the daughter of the incarcerated Fouquet, sent him a brief note. "Dear François, I am having a dinner party today. Do come—among the persons present will be the celebrated Madame Guyon."

I saw Archbishop Fénelon at the party, and I immediately sensed his great interior vitality. But I stopped in silence as I saw his stony, cold eyes turning to me and then quickly turning away. Yet, my persistent friend, the good duchess, putting down her plate, took his arm and guided him over to me as if he were not the celebrated archbishop but her own brother.

"Darling Jeanne, I want you to meet Archbishop Francois Fénelon, whom I know you have heard about. He graduated from that pious and good seminary, Saint-Sulpice."

Sighing, he looked at me, and I knew he saw me as a diseased woman carrying the contagious disease of heresy.

After a pause, I spoke, "I look forward to hearing you preach." Silence, and then I laughed. "Do you speak to those who have been incarcerated?"

Lines appeared between the eyes of the duchess.

Reluctantly, Fénelon smiled, "Our Lord spoke to everyone and so do I."

Then the duchess smiled. "Our Jeanne has some rough edges since she was locked alone in a small room, separated from her daughter. She found something—or, darling, can I be honest? She has lost some manners, but when I am around her, I know she has found God within."

Jumping in with a smile, I explained. "I lost propriety. You know it is the greatest sin."

The duchess rolled her eyes. "Jeanne, would you like some more tea?"

Fénelon looked at me. "Propriety a sin?"

"Do you think it pleases God to worry constantly about appearances? Do you think it pleases God to conform to fancy social systems and not to God? Who has time here for the joy and love that shows us the beauty of salvation?"

He echoed the phrase. "You are right about needing the beauty of salvation."

I persevered in my search for a connection with him. "I want to be a simple person living for Christ: a fool for Christ, as Apostle Paul says in I Corinthians 4:10. That is all I want to be."

Fénelon pursed his lips. "I must go and greet Madame de Maintenon." He bowed slightly, left, and found Maintenon. It was such a complicated social situation with this woman, the secret wife of the king, not publicly acknowledged as the queen of France.

"Madame, how are you doing?"

A renowned spiritual director, his famous gentle eyes now searched hers for any sign of distress or unhappiness.

She allowed herself a quiet sigh. "Louis has not strayed into pastures of other women—at least recently—but I have realized something."

Respectfully Fénelon waited.

"We all need glory—that sense of adventure and drama—that shows us we are important." Fénelon smiled in recognition of the truth that she spoke.

She continued "My life has been filled with glory. I have had the heavy losses of suffering and odd twists of fate. And now as his wife, such an unexpected honor visited upon me." She paused, and chose honesty speaking to this compassionate man. "At first when I heard of Louis' escapades, I became angry about the humiliation of an unfaithful husband. Then I realized it was not the sexual contact he wanted, but the sense of adventure and glory. He wanted human experience, a very profound sense of life, and sadly he sought this in promiscuity. For Louis, without his endless chain of lovers, everything is dull. He needs glory like rich incense that he breathes in and makes him feel real. I realize now that what he needs is spiritual excitement. God's glory is the only one that lasts: To work for the Kingdom of God and serve Church, there is real adventure! So, I need to surround Louis with men and women who understand this, and maybe, maybe, we can bring the Kingdom of God into Versailles."

Fénelon reached for her hand. "You understand this, Madame. The glory of Christ the King needs to settle on our King Louis and work for his redemption. We will begin to pray for this."

As they parted, Fénelon heard infectious laughter from Guyon and her duchess friend. He saw them give a tender and joyful farewell to each other. Suddenly Fénelon remembered the gospel story of the widow's mite and realized that Madame Guyon had given her all for the Christian faith. How had Guyon survived? Great mysteries surrounded her life with a difficult marriage and cruel incarceration, yet she glowed. Maybe she did indeed have a chaste relationship with La Combe—the rumors about them traveling and living together might be only vicious gossip.

The next morning his hand reached to write a note to Madame Guyon. Fénelon paused, waiting. Heaviness hung around him. He could sense some vision—what? Powerful angelic presence and divine purpose ran rapidly through his mind. The glory of God seemed to envelop Madame Guyon. Then—nothing—all was gone. Quickly, he began the note. "My Dear Madame Guyon, please join us for tea this afternoon. I would very much like to talk with you." A sense of peace enveloped him.

I waited for him, radiant after my prayers. Freed from the torment of incarceration, my mind rested; in simplicity I enjoyed Jesus Christ.

Fénelon walked slowly towards me, head bowed. Our eyes met, intensely locking. Then, without any introductory words, we talked openly.

Fénelon began immediately. "I have learned of the possibility of Christ in the interior life. And in you I see this life fulfilled."

Later Fénelon wrote to me, "I do not know what you do to others, but you bring me many benefits. I would be delighted to be silent with you. I must see you before you leave, to speak of God and to be silent in Him at the home of Madame de Maintenon. Arrange a day with her; she will inform me of it. Be sure that I speak to you with complete simplicity."

Anne-Marie questioned me about what was happening. "Mama, who is this Father Fénelon?"

I sat down, smoothing my daughter's wavy hair. She needed an answer. Anne-Marie snuggled next to me in the chair. I began slowly, "Archbishop Fénelon is an important spiritual director at Versailles. I know that many at the court respect him and they desire his wisdom. "

I frowned. "I fear we will need him. God is showing me the help that has already been arranged for us. Who is Father Fénelon? He is our help and protection."

Anne-Marie laughed. "Yes, Mama. I like this priest."

I answered her slowly, "It seems to me that my soul has perfect rapport with him."

Anne-Marie turned back to her studies while I sat, pondering. What would we face in the future?

Growing Friendships

In her apartment at Versailles, Madame de Maintenon welcomed me to tea. After arriving in her apartment for a moment, we rested in a gentle embrace.

"Jeanne, how good you look!"

I laughed. "It is the refreshing sense of being with you, Madame. I know you understand, as I do, the struggles of life. And you too understand the happiness God has for us." We ate our dessert while opening interior doors of intimacy.

Madame de Maintenon started. "Louis is still not interested in seeking God."

"Give him time, Madame. We are talking about such an intense change, a total conversion from his former way of life."

Madame de Maintenon leaned back and sighed. Maybe this marriage to Louis was not a failure, as she feared in her heart. Maybe God was acting and she (the beaten, orphaned child) could learn to trust God.

Turning towards me, she confided about her first marriage, "After all the gossip of being married to Paul Scarron (why, people would ask me if we could make love with his crippled body!) I now am married to a man who I never know what he is doing." And then in a tearful whisper, "Or who he is with."

I touched her hand.

In simplicity I answered, "Dear Madame, I am most sympathetic to you. Please trust God. There is a path planned for you, a safe journey lived in the heart of Christ."

A moment of pleasant trust arrived in the face of Madame de Maintenon's grave uncertainty.

Fénelon joined us later for lunch, asking forgiveness for his late arrival. "Begging your pardon, Madame, the work at Versailles never ends." But even as he politely focused on the king's wife, I felt his spirit reaching out to me.

Madame de Maintenon questioned him, "What is being said about our Catholic Church at Versailles? Have we recovered from the time years ago Louis knelt at the altar to receive communion with his first wife on one side and his mistress on the other?"

Fénelon answered slowly, "Many now seek a purified and stronger church. I hear a vision of the purified church from others at church councils. Sometimes we meet and share our vision of a new church: a church without intrigue, a church that will guide us to God and a new creation. Others in our country, of course, also wish for purification from our corrupt age, such as the Jansenists, who work tirelessly for new commitment. But somehow, their intense moral vision seems to cut out the beauty and joy of God. I turn to the church mystics for spiritual nourishment. But can we hope for a courageous, believing church at Versailles?"

I nodded my head in agreement. "When I was incarcerated, I learned the power of the Spirit to break down walls and build new paths in this life. When the Spirit removes boundaries, there are beautiful places to explore and indeed to adore our beloved Christ."

Fénelon said, "We pray that Louis uses his power wisely and that his legacy lasts forever. I am even now tutoring Louis' grandson to rule wisely and care for his subjects."

Fénelon sat quietly and began a new conversation with me. "A small group of us gathers to pray for a new beginning, to ask for God's actions of the Holy Spirit at Versailles. We have hope, now that Louis has made this quiet marriage to Madame de Maintenon, that possibly he will have a change of heart and learn to seek God's will for this land he rules." He smiled. "I hear we are secretly called the Court Cenacle, meaning the holy group. We in this Court Cenacle understand how crucial these changes are for France." He paused.

"We would like for you to be part of this, Jeanne."

And so it began. In the Court Cenacle, we felt as if the Kingdom of God was entering our lives. Human power and spiritual power might become united, and then anything would be possible. In the Court Cenacle, we enjoyed open dialogue as a trusted group of top advisors to Louis XIV. We prayed for both his salvation and for his power. We encouraged morally courageous state and church leaders. We met regularly at dinner where even servants were not allowed so our conversations would not be overheard.

Who belonged? Archbishop Fénelon, Duc de Chevreuse and his wife; Duc de Beauvilliers and his wife; Madame de Maintenon; and a few others. They all welcomed a fresh vision of the Kingdom of God. I found in this group emotional tenderness, compassion for all persons, elegant spirituality, and beautiful intimacy with Christ. Indeed, this was a golden moment in time!

The Wedding

I pulled the long, white dress over my teenage daughter's head, looking at Anne-Marie's dancing eyes. She twirled around and then reached out to me, pulling me close.

"Mama—what a lovely dress! Thank you for everything."

Happily I looked into Anne-Marie's fresh face and saw hope for the future. Slowly we simultaneously arranged the dress, gave a hug and wiped our eyes, wet with joy.

"Mama, it's time now. Will you put on my wedding veil?"

I lifted rich French lace and adorned my laughing daughter's hair, sparkling with the purity of young life. As together we walked into the church, I prayed that the two young people might be made one. Standing at the altar of Christ, Anne-Marie reached out for her new husband's arm. I saw the goodness of life gracing my daughter's life as she joined with Monsieur L. Nicholas Fouquet, Count de Vaux.

Somehow, behind the lace and wonder, I sensed the joining together of families destined to serve God: de la Mothe, Fouquet, and Guyon. In great relief I knew, Anne-

Marie was safe and in this thought was great rest. My beloved child had found a safe haven and a home.

"My dear Fénelon," I wrote. "God designs love for us. Plans, hopes, and dreams grace our every step if we but believe. When our hopes are disrupted, we are to wait patiently for the new fresh emerging plans of God. But God's ways are built upon our humility, our understanding of our need for God. We expect a certain path and God will have nothing of this. There will be times of uncertainty, not knowing, not understanding, and then we are to have complete trust in the goodness of God. When we are truly lost, when the ways of the world confound us, then we start to live and move and have our being in God. When we look back, we will be horrified at the rough concepts, the restrictive laws, the cruel judgments that we have believed. All the pleasures we have sought are poor, temporary harbors, nothing compared to the glorious, free life of the Spirit of Christ."

François met me at the church door before tea at the home of Madame de Maintenon.

"How is everything, Father?" I asked.

"Jeanne, I am trying to conquer my selfishness, my instincts, my earthly ambitions—just as you suggest. But, my dear tormenter, have you spent days at Versailles trying to belong to God alone?

"I walk around the halls seeing how correctly everyone prances—as if we are in a huge ballet. I hear concerns expressed—are they petty?—how everyone is trying to remain in good standing with the king. I spend hours with the young Duke of Burgundy trying to educate him in a different way of thought: the belief that kings actually serve their subjects." Looking directly at me, he smiled. "Have you tried this, my dear Madame, living in complete luxury and seeking God, and yet not being seduced by the immense power of serving King Louis? And at the end of the day I write my letters, direct and clear, trying to warn others of the lack of moral vision and of the corruption we dwell in day after day."

Father Fénelon paused before continuing. "Do you know what I am like, Jeanne? A winter tree, devoid of leaves and anything green, but then I feel tiny new leaves popping out everywhere. But if I am to be honest, all these new leaves are selfish ambitions, bloom of the enticement of power, a hope for a higher church position, or maybe I could plan powerful projects. So I cut off these ambitious blooms, Jeanne, and what will I have left, my challenging friend? A dead tree." François stops, posing as a dead tree, a strange animation possessing him, a wonder that he finally has expressed his deepest thoughts.

I smiled at his voice's vibrancy. "No, my eloquent friend, you will be a distinguished man listening to and participating in the heavenly hierarchy with angels and archangels."

In jest, the priest bowed toward me. "My dear Madame, the only thing that distinguishes me is that I listen to your preposterous, astounding words. And now, may I accompany you to tea with Madame de Maintenon? Maybe she will encourage these small green leaves of mine."

I laughed, but for a second, saw truth coming through his unexpected words. "Abbe, father, God's designs on you are as apparent as those ambitions you hold so dear. I wonder whether you will choose the ways of God."

"And you, my female author, what will you choose?"

I knew my answer. "Christ alone. After all—what else is there? God has given us such delights, friendship, love, warm tea. Let's go—I look forward to the fresh fruit pastries."

A few weeks later I walked into my daughter's kitchen to see my son-in-law Nicholas kissing my Anne-Marie. I backed out of the kitchen; what had I written about in my commentary on the Song of Solomon? The kisses of God begin our journey with God. We start towards union with God with glorious kisses, warm and intriguing.

Later returning, I saw Anne-Marie stirring the rich stew simmering over the fire. "Oh, Mama, come and taste. Should we add more spices?"

I took the spoon my daughter offered me. "Yes, my little one. I still can't believe that you are a wife."

Anne-Marie giggled. "Nor I, my Mama. Have you seen the apple cake?"

I hugged her. "I puzzle about many things, silly child of mine, but none is more mysterious to me than how you turned out to be a wonderful cook. What did I feed you growing up, child? I cannot even bear to remember."

Anne-Marie stopped. "No you are the silly one, my unusual Mama. We ate wonderfully fresh bread, warm cheese, apples off the trees, grapes off the vine. I learned about the fresh produce and wanted to cook it to show off its glories."

I walked over to the heavy oak table to cut the bread. As I reached for a piece of the warm bread, the door opened and Archbishop Fénelon entered.

François started. "My Jeanne, what an evening we share! Anne-Marie's first dinner party."

Briefly, our eyes met.

Nicholas entered. "Father Fénelon, what an honor that you would visit our home."

"I hope to come often. You and your beautiful bride Anne-Marie are like children to me. Would you accept me as an honorary uncle? I do hope I can join with your family."

Nichols swallowed. "My dear Father, we do not deserve this honor, but I accept this joy openly. You have an open invitation to our home."

Anne-Marie struggled in the door, trying to carry glasses, and Nicholas ran over to help.

Then turning back to the archbishop, Nicholas asked. "Please grace our house with a toast, Father."

François bowed his head. "Our loving God, you made your first miracle at a wedding in Cana when the marriage feast ran out of wine. I pray a blessing for this young couple: may their love run fresh and pure, may their marriage bless everyone around them, and may Anne-Marie and Nicholas become one in you, our ultimate joy. And now we remember before you, God, the poor, the hungry, the suffering, and may our lives reach out to them and minister to them."

We raised our glasses with real contentment.

Anne-Marie suggested, "And may we bless my Mama, Father Fénelon?"

Fénelon paused, saying simply. "To the woman who already receives the heavenly feast and makes it ours even now."

The quiet family raised glasses towards me and, to my surprise, tears ran down my cheeks.

At times the Spirit is so much fun; how quickly, how merrily, the spiritual journey sinks into our hearts.

VII
Tumultuous Times

Rumors at Versailles swirled like dead leaves caught in a dry wind. After I had written so many of my books about prayer and interior faith, I began to hear of others who speak of knowing Christ in this lifetime. Rumors began to circulate that the Spanish priest Miguel Molinos told people of the possibility of a deep and satisfying relationship with Christ. Living at the Vatican, he radiated joy and energy, and many were drawn to him, even the pope. In the quiet, Molinos said, God gives us divine substance and meaning.

Some called him heretical. It became a very dangerous thing even to say his name. Molinos spoke a simple message about the presence of Christ and soon this belief that Christ lived within us became increasingly controversial in Europe.

The sunlight shone in the window as I sat pondering this.

Now the Court Cenacle began to realize that King Louis felt our growing power and our emerging spirituality. The struggles against my theology intensified. *A Short and Easy Method of Prayer* was placed on the Catholic Index of Condemned Books on November 29, 1689.

I had learned that when we make ourselves available to Christ, soon there would be a time to minister in the name of Christ and a situation of testing. This would not come without a cost. Soon this time fell on the Court Cenacle.

One day Fénelon took the luxury of walking amidst the Versailles gardens. A small stumbling boy ran up to him. As Francois turned to the sound of his urgent whisper, he felt chills.

"Father! Good father, I have been waiting to see you."

Francois leaned over and recognized the too-short malnourished body of a teenager.

"Yes, my child? What can I do for you?"

The boy grabbed at him, almost falling. "My mother just died."

Francois steadied the boy. "God be with her soul! Tell me more."

"My brothers can't walk, my father is weak, but he told me to find the good Father, not the other ones, and ask you to please come."

Francois felt an inner shrinking for a second, and then he leaned forward. "Yes, of course, where?"

"To the village over the river near the closed mill."

Fénelon pictured the geography, remembering the way.

"Yes. Let me get my carriage and give you a ride."

Relieved tears sprang forth. "Food? Will you bring bread?"

Fénelon's eyes grew strong. "Of course."

An hour later the boy and the priest arrived in the village.

"They are dying, good Father. All of them."

Fénelon moved closer to the boy. "You mean all your family?"

"No, all the villagers. We have nothing left. Look—they are all dead."

Fénelon, squinting his eyes, saw little huts with utter stillness. A bizarre stillness lay on everything: no one walking, no dogs barking, no farm animals.

"Where did they go?"

The boy whispered, "Go, good Father? Does no one talk about this? They lie dead inside."

Fénelon tapped at the carriage window. "Stop, Monsieur."

He jumped out of the carriage and started running over the fields, his black cassock outstretched in the breeze.

He came to the first hut. "Monsieur? Madame?"

Hearing nothing he walked in. There on the floor lay two small bodies of children. On top of them lay an emaciated corpse of a woman, her hands on the head of the bald, dead infant, her eyes looking up, hopeless, cold.

Fénelon instinctively bent down. Was he too late? Yes, cold. At his gentle touch, her head fell and mouth opened . He cried out, for stuffed in her mouth was unchewed grass.

The boy spoke. "Father, please let us go. My family waits like this. All around here, they are dead. We have no food."

Fénelon stood up and felt a cloud-like presence of the Spirit. No, his heart screamed!

"Please, Abbe. Let us go." Running, Fénelon returned to the carriage, his pastoral fire making him tense, alert, watching.

"Go quickly, sit up beside the driver, tell him where. If we can save one life, then God is still here."

The boy pointed and yelled as he came finally to another hut. Not waiting for the carriage to stop, he grabbed bread, jumping off and running, "Daddy! Hold on. We are here."

At the entrance, the same tangled heap of bodies, yet this time, weak eyes turned towards the sound of his beloved child.

"Daddy! Here, eat a bite and wait to see if you can swallow."

The father, now the child to his son, obediently took a bite and struggled to chew.

"Wait, my child, I will be back." Fénelon murmured. He placed all the food down that they had brought and strode back to the carriage. "Versailles immediately." Jeanne would help, the Court Cenacle would help.

Quickly, Fénelon asked his driver. "How many? How long?"

The driver struggled to speak the words of truth. "I can't count how many villages, Abbe. The poor everywhere are...." And waiting tears sprang from him.

"Let us hurry."

Fénelon sat back and started planning.

Versailles was in a hub-bub getting ready for another Moliere play. Then the shocking information from Fénelon arrived.

I received his note and ran to the kitchen. How much flour, how many vegetables, anything dried? And I started asking others to help.

Fénelon approached the good dukes of the Court Cenacle. One of them asked, What could we do, where can we go? Who was Louis sleeping with now that took all of his time?

Distracted, Fénelon barely heard the question directed at him.

"Yes, I have heard about the new play at Versailles. The king sponsored it and wants us all to attend. Will I be at Madame de Maintenon's dinner party?" He shook his head no, smiled gently and walked away.

Touching his arm lightly, the Duc de Chevreuse stopped him. Fénelon stood alert, sensing danger. They communicated in abbreviated phrases.

"Have you told the king?"

"I have some drafts of this already written." Fénelon flinched at the memory of difficult hours drafting this letter.

The duke began. "It is growing, Father. The reports come in daily. Yet Louis is either fox-hunting or following his theatrical or romantic pursuits."

Immediately Fénelon responded. "It is time. Enough. I will send this letter to him immediately."

The duke walked away without a word.

Archbishop Fénelon spoke from the heart of pure love. In 1693 Fénelon sent the letter to King Louis XIV over which he had toiled so mightily.

"Sire, he who takes upon himself the liberty of thus addressing you has no interests to serve in this world. . . . If he speaks to you bluntly, be not dismayed, for truth at all times is strong and free... .

"Thus it is that your people, whom you should love as your own children and who have hitherto so passionately loved you, are now dying of hunger. Cultivation is almost at a standstill, population in town and country is falling, trades of all kinds are dying out and producing ever fewer workmen; commerce is non-existent. Thus you have destroyed virtually half of the inner strength of the country in order to undertake and maintain useless conquests beyond its frontiers. Instead of extracting ever more money from your poor people, you ought to be giving it to them to buy food. The magistrate is despised and worn out. The nobility, whose hold on their possessions is by decree, live entirely on the State, while you are harassed by a crowd of greedy and importunate hangers-on. But it is you yourself, Sire, who have brought all these troubles upon your own head since, while the kingdom is in ruins, you keep what there is in your own hands, and no one can live except upon your bounty. And this is that great kingdom so prosperous under a monarch who is always depicted as the joy of the people and who indeed would be so if flattering advice had not poisoned him!

The letter was signed François Fénelon. Yet the famine of 1693-1694 claimed about six hundred thousand lives of the forgotten peasants.

Now Louis knew that Fénelon and others in the Court Cenacle were courageous enough to speak out. The Sun King contemplated his future actions against them, and Madame de Maintenon became pulled in two opposing directions.

The Fateful Intersection

I saw the growing tensions of the coming historical intersection of events. Versailles, Madame de Maintenon's school at St. Cyr, and the Vatican began their fateful intersection. I pondered the unusual narration of this history.

Versailles

"I will not have it! This is an affront to my power." Louis called in his personal Jesuit confessor, Father de la Chaise. "Get that Spanish priest Miguel Molinos condemned."

The priest bowed in assent. "King," he began, "I recognize the dangers of this Quietism in destroying the church order that you have helped the Jesuits build in France."

Louis interrupted. "I know the pope refused to condemn Molinos' theology one time before. I will be satisfied only with this man destroyed. Tell that to the pope. Look at Molinos' writings saying that everyone can have union with God. I will have problems with my subjects if they start saying that God talks to them. Go to the pope and return with the news that Molinos is destroyed."

And the confessing priest left, plans running through his head on how to get the pope to agree with this condemnation.

The School at St. Cyr

Madame de Maintenon walked into her school at St. Cyr, where daughters of impoverished nobleman attended. She affectionately placed her hand on the head of one rambunctious teenager speaking loudly, and said, "Gently, Brigitte, gently." The girl smiled and slowed down. Others ran up to their patroness, smiling, anticipating rewards from her.

Madame de Maintenon sat in her favorite rocking chair. "I have a special treat for you today. I have brought a very special woman in for you to meet. Madame Guyon has written a powerful book, *The Short and Easy Method of Prayer*. She will teach you about it. I am sure this prayer will help you in your future life." And Madame de Maintenon thought again of the anguished life of poverty and possibly prostitution that she hoped these girls would avoid.

I smiled at these teenagers. "There is a future for you, girls. A good one that God will bless you with. Now let us start in prayer, with each one of us looking inside for God."

Brigitte questioned. "Madame, I have my rosary here. Is that what you want us to do?"

I answered quietly. "No, child. I am talking about a different prayer. God wants our hearts and souls. Look for God within your heart, quietly, knowing that Christ dwells within you."

After the class, Madame de Maintenon walked out, her head upright, "I must go find Father Fénelon. Surely he will understand now that he must persuade Louis to crown me as Queen of France so I may have more power to continue doing these good works."

The Vatican

At the Vatican, the wind blew wildly as Father de la Chaise walked up to the meeting with Pope Innocent XII in St. Peter's Basilica. He practiced the words he would say and soon his audience with the pope began.

"Pope, I bring you respectful words from King Louis XIV. He will not be satisfied with anything less than full condemnation of this heretical doctrine of Miguel Molinos. He is committed to driving heresy out of France. And, Pope, he sends you word that he is actively supporting you in all of your efforts to destroy the heretical Protestants also. He asks if you need any further assistance in these important efforts."

The pope sighed. What countries had broken off from his papacy with this cancerous growth of Protestantism: parts of Germany, England, the Netherlands, and more. Flushing, the pope stopped the ambassador from speaking anymore. "I understand your communication, Father. You may leave."

After a grand bow, the Jesuit priest turned and left.

The pope slumped some in his throne. Then turning to his assistant he said softly, "Please have the cardinals judge the theology of Miguel Molinos. And cancel all of my future engagements with Molinos."

The pope tensed as he remembered the laughter and the engaging faith of his good friend and knew that the nuns Molinos directed would be devastated. Yet the pope could not think of this because of the dire consequences. If King Louis took France away from the Catholic Church, what would be left? Gripping his fist together, the pope decided this friendship must end.

The pope sat erect, frozen in time.

Versailles

Madame de Maintenon turned to Archbishop Fénelon. "How is your tutoring of the Duke of Burgundy going, Father? Louis has the highest confidence in you to allow your tutoring of his grandson. We all hope he will be a wise monarch one day."

"I am training him in the ancient path of wisdom. He progresses well."

"Father, we all hope for a purified, spiritual France. And now I must ask your help with Louis. I insisted on an honorable marriage, but Louis demanded this be done quietly with only three witnesses. Now I see that I must be proclaimed Queen of France in order that all can be influenced by our power. Think of the good we could all do if I were queen, Father."

François Fénelon looked at Madame de Maintenon. "I will pray about this, Madame." And leaving her apartment at Versailles, he felt his mind racing, leaping, struggling towards divine wisdom, for chaos approached.

Vatican

The famed spiritual director Miguel Molinos wrote, "The depth of our spirit, you must know, is the place of our happiness. There the Lord shows us wonders. There we move and lose ourselves in the immeasurable sea of His infinite goodness, and in it we abide steadfast and immovable. There resides the incomparable fruit of the spirit, and the wonderful and sweet quiet. The humble and resigned Christian who has reached this depth seeks now only the fulfilling of God's will, and the divine and loving Spirit teaches all things with His sweet and vivifying unction."

In July 1685, Miguel heard the knock at his small study as he sat quietly writing. He opened the door to see guards waiting for him. "You are being arrested," barked the brusque order.

Miguel paled. Then he tensed, and turning to his desk, slowly closed his latest work, and with peaceful resignation quietly walked towards the guards.

Father de la Chaise smiled indulgently when the messenger brought news of Molinos' incarceration. "That is just the beginning. Now we want public humiliation of this heretic, so the people know what happens to those who are led astray by his thinking."

The messenger stoically nodded. He knew his sister, the nun, would be horrified.

Father de la Chaise continued. "Now take that heretic's letters to the court of the Inquisition, and we will see who else we can bring to God's righteous judgment."

The powerful priest rubbed his hands rapidly back and forth, back and forth, like the swishing of a sword.

School at St. Cyr

I walked in the next day, planning my new spiritual lessons with my students.

"Madame, I want to be a nanny!" Brigitte exclaimed.

"A most honorable profession," I encouraged.

"And I, Madame, I would like to teach," another exclaimed. Her enthusiasm made me smile. "All of you are a joy to me. We are making progress."

I was aware of the growing international intrigue as I contentedly look at my young charges. "My little ones, the world is a rough place for the poor. Some of you will marry and have security, but some of you won't. But God will never desert you. Now that you know how to pray, realize that you are given the power to live with peace and joy. God will always show you a way through your struggles."

Brigitte sat straight. Because of Christ within, she was not afraid. She had goals and plans. She reached out to me with an impulsive hug.

Vatican

The church officials told the poor to go to the square in front of St. Peter's Basilica at noon. There they would see a prisoner and chant "Condemn him! Condemn!" over and over. They would receive indulgences for their sins and the sins of those they loved, followed by secret rewards of money. They led Miguel Molinos out in chains. He looked around at the crowds and heard them yelling his name, taunting him over and over. He bowed his head in prayer, and quietly looking at his feet, he waited.

Then the dungeon in the basement awaited him again, and he knew not how long. Torture and death could come at any time.

Versailles

Madame de Maintenon led the Bishop of Chartres Godot in to see her spiritual daughters. "Madame Guyon, the close friend of Father Fénelon, has tutored them in prayer."

The Bishop frowned. Then he saw self-confident young women standing quietly waiting for him. They stood looking directly at him, self-possessed. "Here begins trouble," he realized. No docile, submissive teenagers here. Looking at Madame de Maintenon, he wondered, "Does she know what she has done?" He must talk to her immediately.

In the meantime, Father Fénelon wrote Madame de Maintenon, "I must see you. I do not think your plan to have yourself declared Queen of France is a good one. Your ego is your unbroken idol, Madame." Madame de Maintenon crumpled the note, remembering her poverty-stricken family and her panicked mother. And now another betrayal confronted her. But she knew how to get revenge. She had power over his friend, Madame Guyon. But, I will watch for a season, she pondered, the time must be right.

School at St. Cyr

And Madame de Maintenon entered an order May 2, 1693, saying Madame Guyon was never to be allowed at the School of St. Cyr again.

Versailles

Archbishop Fénelon wrote, "Dear Jeanne, "I must see you immediately. This situation with the Bishop of Chartres is escalating. I fear you will be arrested. Would you agree to invite the Bishop Bossuet into this? I believe that he will help us because he is a spiritual man. After the condemnation of Miguel Molinos, we need to recognize what a serious situation this is. Unfortunately Louis XIV may seek more and more condemnations of the spiritual life. Father La Combe is still incarcerated, and now Father Molinos. Who will be next?"

A meeting was planned between Bishop Bossuet and Archbishop Fénelon.

Bossuet entered the drawing room to see Fénelon waiting for him. He paused and with affection looked at the tall archbishop. This student Fénelon had done so well and Bossuet had found such joy in consecrating him as an archbishop. Bishop Bossuet thought, "I knew this man would have a distinguished career. I saw his gifts so clearly. A brilliant mind, a wise heart, and tender love: his aristocratic heritage created this wonderful priest."

Francois looked up and reverently waited for Bishop Bossuet to begin.

"Fénelon, how good of you to wait for me! Today has been constant meetings about the spiritual life. One day, Francois, I think much of this responsibility will be yours. Or maybe you will prefer becoming a cardinal at the Vatican: the pope needs someone as wise as you."

Francois briefly smiled at the thought of the intellectual, spiritual life in the elegant Roman church.

"But, my son, I have come to caution you about your friendship with Madame Guyon. She claims that Christ is within people. Please, Francois, do this for me and for the church: distance yourself from this unbalanced woman. There is talk around here, my son."

Francois paled, understanding the implication.

"Bishop, could we meet about this? I have read the writings of Madame Guyon. They are full of Christian faith; they remind me always of the good church mystics."

Bishop Bossuet frowned. "There are always problems with spiritual Christians. They are inherently unstable people. If you insist, I will look at these writings, but understand, Francois, regular church order needs a strong, orthodox hierarchy. Do not be too open with the lay people. It is not good for you or for me—indeed, for the priesthood.

My son, these people who talk of their prayer corrupt our holy priesthood."

Francois walked slowly away from his meeting with Bishop Bossuet. He strolled the halls at Versailles before he returned to his apartment. All you have to do is look at their eyes, he thought, to see their vanities. Hardened in lust, they looked at one before they change to another partner. When they tire of this one, they leave behind tears from those who unfortunately fell into love.

In January, 1694, Bishop Bossuet visited me.

"Here is everything I have written," I said quietly. And I handed the illustrious Bishop Bossuet my finished Autobiography along with my other writings.

The Bishop nodded. "For your protection, please come and stay at a convent in Meaux for this winter while I read your writings. Father Fénelon and I will gather together a group of learned theologians and bishops to read your writings." And so the Issy conferences began and lasted through 1695. The group of learned theologians debated and argued about the work of Christian mystics in the church, including reading all of my writings.

All of the participants at the Issy conferences signed a document saying that some religious experiences need to be left to the judgment of God alone. An example of an unusual religious experience not understood by many was that of the innocent sufferings of Job.

After my arrival at Meaux, though, I realized that this was not a visit, but really an incarceration.

When Bishop Bossuet arrived at the nunnery where I stayed, the nuns were singing a song to the incarnation of Christ. He entered my small room where I sit quietly reading. "I have read everything you have written. You are a deluded woman, but we can finish this affair if you sign this document saying that you do not believe in the incarnation. Then I will say you have agreed to my judgment, have submitted to the church, and I will let you go free. I will also clear your reputation again."

I stated clearly, "I know how to do many things, Bishop, but I do not know how to lie. Of course I believe in the incarnation; I live dedicated to Jesus."

Bishop Bossuet responded, "Who are you, an uneducated woman, to challenge me, a bishop? You will sign this document."

I answered, "The Lord worked through Balaam's ass when it was necessary. If God could work through an ass, surely God could also work through a woman."

Bishop Bossuet walked angrily out of the door, pushing past the waiting nun.

Returning to his palatial Versailles apartment, he wrote a note to the mother superior at Meaux. "Let Madame Guyon leave." If Guyon was out, she would surely seek the company of Fénelon quickly. The famous Bishop stopped, frowning, his eyes intense. "I need to make sure that Louis sees the unhealthy relationship that Fénelon has with that woman.

As soon as the order was put in allowing me to leave, I gathered my things and left in the presence of some good friends.

The struggles against my theology intensified. On October 16, 1694, the Archbishop of Paris Harlay condemned my books, *A Short and Easy Method of Prayer* and *Commentary on Song of Songs*. On August 6, 1695, Archbishop Harlay died suddenly while walking in the Parisian gardens with one of his lovers.

Catastrophe hit when Madame de Maintenon wanted to be named Queen and the Cenacle did not support this. Our group was torn apart, and soon some were thrown out of Versailles. And I wondered about my former friend: why, Madame de Maintenon, why did you betray us?

Maybe Maintenon had already betrayed herself too many times.

Madame de Maintenon welcomed Bishop Bossuet to her apartment at Versailles.

"Thank you for your time," the Bishop said courteously.

Maintenon jumped into the subject of the desired prestigious position of Archbishop of Paris. "Archbishop Harlay's unexpected death has shocked us all, and to die in the presence of his paramour has left the church once again with a stained reputation. Louis and I believe that the next prelate who has this position must have a personal life beyond reproach," she stated bluntly.

"The Lord has a way of making our deaths fit the circumstances of our lives. Yes, the life of the next archbishop cannot have the indiscretions of Archbishop Harlay," Bossuet said carefully.

Maintenon smiled. "Of course you are right about the death." She pushed her hair back from her face. "I am gathering names for Louis even now for this important church position." She paused. "But I have one lingering problem, and that is that heretic Guyon."

They both paused.

Maintenon talked in a stronger voice. "She must be condemned; her books have spread heresies. If the church stops her, then Archbishop Fénelon will realize how wrong he is about that woman. She deserves the scaffold or the fire."

Immediately seeing the implications, the Bishop nodded. Destroying Guyon would be an important first step in destroying Fénelon, his closest rival for the archbishop of Paris. This would be an easy political maneuver: destroy Guyon's reputation and, like a domino, Fénelon's would go also. Bossuet thought, "Clearly, the people in Paris need my steady hand for spiritual guidance; think about the chaos that would develop under the spiritual excesses of the unstable Fénelon. Hadn't he tried to reach Fénelon before he destroyed himself with Guyon?" Bossuet felt his own conscience clean of any guilt about this conspiracy.

Without expressing his interior ideas, Bossuet replied in simplicity, "Certainly, Madame." He leaned over, kissed her hand and gave her a lingering look. "All of France benefits from your wisdom."

Surely then, Bossuet thought, Fénelon would never be made Archbishop of Paris. And who could Louis, under the advice of Madame de Maintenon, appoint but me?"

Madame de Maintenon entered King Louis' room. "I need your help and need to confess what has happened, King. There is a heresy at St. Cyr. I am afraid Madame Guyon has corrupted these young women."

Louis stood up, saying coldly to the guards, "Remove Madame de Maintenon immediately. And do not approach me again. A heresy in my court? Never! Archbishop Fénelon is banished from my court. Draw up an order of arrest against this Madame Guyon. And find Bishop Bossuet so that I can learn how this heresy spread so rapidly. He should have informed me about this earlier."

Soon Louis appointed Louis Antoine Noailles, Madame de Maintenon's close friend, as the new Archbishop of Paris. Quickly after this appointment, the new archbishop Noailles understood that Fénelon was a political liability and also broke his friendship with Fénelon. Louis' court understood the significance of these actions: Noailles wanted only to please Louis and appear proper to everyone.

Father Fénelon wrote me, "Run, Jeanne. They are coming to arrest you."

VIII
Arrest and Vincennes

I sat alone in my small room. This was not a time to betray the wisdom of Christ. I prayed, "My God, my Father, the letters are arriving—from many sources—telling me to run, informing me of the decision of Louis to arrest me. They ask me to leave not only my home, but my country. They tell me of others who have fled France seeking for religious safety. These good people seek a new life in England and the "New World".

"Run? Leave France?" Tears chaotically sprang onto my cheeks.

"I know incarceration and I know how evil it is. I want no more of this!" My clenched hands vainly tried to stop the river of water raging from my eyes.

Then I quickly stood up. "I feel I am not called to start a new world but to minister to this one. Father, could I leave the land of the River Loire, of the Cathedral of Notre Dame? My children were born and baptized here." My prayer continued.

"Jesus stayed for the confrontation with evil. He had been told that Herod the fox was after him, and yet he did not run. Indeed, as the Scripture says, Jesus headed into Jerusalem and faced into the murderous intentions of the temple leaders."

I thought carefully and slowly. "There is a time for confrontations. There is a moment when we need to say to the powers of evil that there is a power within us greater than the evil: that is, my inward Christ whom I met so many years ago. And somehow, I know not why, I feel called to stay in my homeland and see what happens in the clash between the force of Louis XIV and Christ.

"But, my Lord, descend as justice in my life. I do not want your mercy but your justice. I long for the righteousness of the burning bush, the heavenly vision of the transfiguration, and the power of the resurrection. And if Christ's justice calls for my incarceration and suffering and allows the violence of the state, so be it."

And these final words of decision were choked by tears.

King Louis attacked. He aimed his powerful political machine at those practicing interior prayer, for he believed that these Christian powers must be destroyed. Prayerful

Christians, he decided, hindered his goal of becoming the universal monarch—the most powerful King of all time. In his mind the spiritual gifts of Guyon, and Fénelon tarnished the golden splendor of his brilliant court. No mercy would be shown these unsightly heretics, who like ugly blotches marred the brightness of the Sun King.

At Versailles the thirteen-year-old Duke of Burgundy walked in to see his father Louis XIV.

"I have heard that you banished my teacher, Archbishop Fénelon. Please, sire, do not take him away. I have learned so much from him. He talks to me about when I become the King of France and how I will follow just laws, as do the royal subjects."

Louis frowned. "You will be the total authority, not follow laws. This is dangerous doctrine Fénelon is teaching you. I know your love for this priest, and because of this I will not incarcerate this respected archbishop. But this man Fénelon will be condemned to banishment to the diocese of Cambray. Never will he be allowed in Versailles again to cause trouble in my court."

The boy trembled convulsively.

"I will find a new tutor for you who will help you get over these strange ideas."

Mute, the boy walked out after his dismissal.

The vision of the purified leadership was corrupted and dying. Now our Court Cenacle was torn apart.

Sweat glistened on the archbishop's forehead as he wrote a furtive note to me.

"We had been so close. The Duke of Burgundy—so young and yet so wise. The Court Cenacle—so intelligent and so powerful—is now broken and dying. And then Madame de Maintenon lets it be known that she will intercede with Louis if I ask for your condemnation. Maintenon said you were a regrettable mistake and you should be destroyed."

I sat frozen as I read the note, but I heard other rumors; and these words brought chills of wonder to me. I heard that my friend Fénelon was writing a book defending me. Instead of bowing to pressure, he wrote a book that I was told was titled *The Maxims of the Saints*. I pondered in amazement: this man would help me instead of saving himself.

Fénelon's theology flowed passionately as he wrote to defend me. My nun cousin Elise, still working at St. Cyr, wrote to tell me what happened.

The elegant archbishop paced around his study. What do I need to say, he wondered? He began his book *The Maxims of the Saints*. The pure love of Christ calls to us, yet only a few respond to this call. Pure love accepted no compromises and allowed no self-interest.

Fénelon wrote his book with vivid details. What was this journey of pure love like? A believer with some struggle traveled up a high mountain. On the top of this mountain, the believer saw another mountain peak, looking inviting. On this second mountain peak dwelled the glorious Kingdom of Heaven, and the believer desired to get there. Looking from one mountain peak to another, they seemed so close to each other: why, there was heaven lived with a gracious sense of hope. And the believer said to the second mountain peak, there is my home! There is where I belong—right over there! Standing on one mountain of human achievement and looking directly at the second one, the distance appeared easily journeyed.

Fénelon wrote, "That is what our experience of the Kingdom of Heaven is like. The Christian affirmed, the

Kingdom of Heaven is right there! As the Bible says, God is nearer than our breath. Let us go there and dwell in Christ's purpose.

"So the journey began. The believer started the journey heading down the first mountain peak to get to the base of the second mountain. And traveling down, immediately there were strange caves and unusual valleys. The believer stepped on sharp rocks and found dangerous cliffs. At times he fell and hurt himself. And now the second mountain, the Kingdom of Heaven seemed so far away.

"Then the Christian stopped to pray and to understand. Why all this danger and struggle? The vision of Heaven is so close, yet the journey so protracted. At one moment the person might cry out 'My God, my God, why hast thou forsaken me?'"

Fénelon paced around as he wrote.

"And at that moment the person experienced an utter abandonment to God and rested on the height of complete faith. Then the person became one with God and as flexible as a feather flying in the Spirit's wind. The Spirit makes the person as clear as a pool of untroubled water. The surrender to God allowed the person to receive the Kingdom of Heaven.

"The believer loved purely then. As the costly journey unfolded, pure love enveloped, consoled, and guided. Through the energy of the spirit, the person continued the journey to the mountain peak of the Kingdom of Heaven.

"Christians declared throughout the ages, 'The vision is real and the only way to heaven is to live in abandoned trust and pure love. God provides food along the way through beautiful, glowing hope. 'The vision is real and the Kingdom of Heaven is realized in unseen ways. Look at Job. The Church overlooks the highly unusual religious experience of this suffering man. But maybe"—and Fénelon leaned closer as he wrote—"maybe suffering is the necessary ingredient that we all want to overlook and to deny.

"But what has the believer found but loving God in simplicity and faith? These are the treasures of the spiritual life!"

Archbishop Fénelon published these ideas in his *Maxims of the Saints* in 1697.

The court at Versailles murmured angrily about this spiritual approach to this controversy. Who can understand this, the nobles criticized. Nobody loves purely; what Archbishop Fénelon was saying is utter foolishness.

Suffering that God may visit upon us—never would that happen!

Louis called for Father de la Chaise again, once again seeing clearly that this theology challenged his authority.

"Tell the pope to condemn Archbishop Fénelon and his heretical writings."

Father de la Chaise left for the Vatican, reflecting on Fénelon's well-known devotion to the pope. What would it take to destroy Fénelon's reputation in Rome? Of course, he thought, Fénelon was vulnerable because of his friendship with Madame Guyon.

Bishop Bossuet also reacted furiously to the *Maxims of the Saints* by writing his response called Quakerism á-la-Mode.

In graphic terms, Bossuet insulted me, including references to my body.

He recommended capital punishment. "Guyon should be sent to the scaffold to be hung until dead or to the fire to be burned alive." He continued, "Archbishop Fénelon has been so foolish we should condemn him also."

For Bossuet's service, Louis poured generous gifts of money and honor upon this receptive priest who was loudly proclaiming the divine right of the king. Next Louis asked the pope to condemn Fénelon.

Many talked about the scene at the Vatican.

The King's confessor, Father de la Chaise was received by the pope who started the conversation. "So now you come seeking the condemnation of my respected Archbishop Fénelon? This priest is an intellectual genius from a long and distinguished French family."

The priest shrugged. "We have all heard the stories of this man and his belief in pure love. King Louis will have none of this mystic contamination at Versailles."

The pope looked off in the distance. "I will appoint a committee of cardinals to decide this one." And he quietly prayed that this committee would have the wisdom of Solomon.

Louis continued his aggression against us.

Next Bishop Bossuet sent out a lettre de cachet, a secret letter, directing incarceration without trial for me.

I now had troubles on every side. What should I do, now that the entire power of the state shot at me?

I heard the news from my friends trying to help: the authorities were coming for me again. My soul screamed in anguish. Running for my room, pushing everything away, I grabbed a few belongings. I fled for the only sanctuary I felt Christ allowed me, a poor section of Paris. Let them leave me alone, I prayed over and over again. I would hide among the poor suffering ones.

I found a small apartment and took new names for me and my two servants. We stayed inside day and night, creeping outside once a week for food and a quick mass at the Cathedral of Notre Dame. With my Master Jesus, I now knew the contempt of the world brought about by the royal court. Bossuet, Maintenon and others needed me to be guilty so they would not appear unjust. Madame de Maintenon could then continue her plan to be proclaimed as the Queen of France.

Yet it was not God's plan to let me escape.

My maid, while arranging to get furniture moved into our hideaway, was recognized and arrested. The policeman Desgrez ordered, "Search her!" In her pocket he found our small key and quickly the orders flew out.

"Take us to Madame Guyon."

Sighing and hanging her head, my servant led them to the small apartment where quietly Desgrez used the key to let himself in, along with a large group of about twenty-five soldiers.

I lay in the small Parisian room sick. Suddenly a claustrophobic feeling struck me—then quietly a tall man entered my room and I, knowing what was coming, resigned myself to what was going to happen. He asked simply, "Are you Madame Guyon?"

Quietly, I answered. "Yes, I am."

"We have you surrounded. Come in!" he called out to the others.

To my amazement, twenty armed soldiers crowded up the stairs. One soldier yelled, "The rest can stay outside."

"Search her and her maid."

How many men did it take to arrest me, Lord? My second incarceration had started with my arrest on December 27, 1695, ordered directly by Bishop Bossuet and Louis XIV, King of France.

I understood this was my sacrifice, and I felt generous consolation in my surrender. I gave all to Christ and waited for His help. I would need divine assistance, for they took me to a large French prison. High on a country hill outside of Paris stood an immense stone château, a castle, surrounded by a wide moat with flowing water and a thick stone wall. Inside the walls presided immense gray towers and long mysterious buildings and permanent stones everywhere. French flags flew showing the power and the authority of the state arrayed against me. Vincennes was their prison of choice to punish me, their accused female criminal.

This was the Vincennes, the place of judgment, and I was being taken to the Keep which was to keep me quiet. I would be emptied of human comfort in this place of hidden torture and isolation. Soldiers with impassive faces were now my surroundings.

The police took prisoners to the Vincennes who questioned Louis' power. I was now officially and authoritatively out of reach. I had heard the rumors of what happened in this prison filled with dreaded torturers and painful interrogations. But I knew the scriptures: what had the Apostle Peter said in I Peter 4:13? "You are participating in the sufferings of Christ."

When I entered for the government admission, I waited quietly.

I heard a soldier mutter to another, "When does she start screaming and crying like all women do coming in here?"

The young man answered, "She doesn't even seem close to tears." He paused. "I wonder what she did. Remember the last woman: after the torture she was screaming for days. This one will be the same."

I turned to them. "I am ready. God will protect me in this place. I thank you for your help."

I walked with dignity. Staring at me, the first soldier whispered, "Maybe God is with her."

After interviewing me and going through my possessions, he called me a liar and said I would be kept away from other prisoners. Turning to the other guards, he added, "Lock her away quickly. This is an extremely dangerous woman."

They put me in one of the darkest cells in Vincennes. Through the gift of resignation, I quickly settled down into a pattern of prayer and devotion with my faithful servant Marie. I sang fervently and enthusiastically, and when I sang, the stones of my tower seemed like rubies. And in the dense darkness of my cell, this place with little light, I found the spiritual light of joy, given to me by my Master Jesus.

Yet, even with my surrender, I found the isolation of the cell painful. The guard would only come by twice a day, once in the morning and again in the evening. One evening I became sick and fell into a coma. I felt very weak and my body grew limp in the dark prison cell. As if from a long distance, I heard Marie standing at the door yelling down the empty halls. "Please, please, I beg you, come and help us."

It seemed to me as if the walls were falling in on me like broken twigs, and I longed to break open the bars and flee from this horror. I fainted.

Then covered with sweat and blood, I took a breath while Marie fell to her knees in relief. I still lived.

Shortly afterwards the long hours of interrogation began.

The very famous Chief of Police de La Reynie shuffled through the many papers he carried into the interrogation, as he looked for evidence that would catch me, their accused criminal, off guard.

"One by one, Madame, we will go through these names and soon the facts of your guilt will emerge."

His austere face showed granite determination.

I looked and caught a glimpse of carefully created documents with a long list of persons I had known.

La Reynie started the interrogation. "Madame, I bring you letters we found in your apartment. Of course we have done a complete investigation. Who are they from?"

"Mainly from my children and Father La Combe."

"Tell us everything in the letters."

Careful, Jeanne. He is trying to make you upset. Remember the face of Jesus. I breathed more slowly and managed a smile.

"Father La Combe is a gifted priest who offered spiritual direction to many."

"Madame, we have another sentence from this heretical priest written to you: "The Jansenists are on top.""

"I am not a Jansenist, Monsieur, and neither is Father La Combe."

La Reynie frowned and I wondered if he was a member of this strongly moral group.

"Monsieur, do you have a mother? For the sake of your mother please watch what you say to me."

La Reynie froze as he remembered his own mother standing before him. He then changed the tactic.

"Father La Combe is a heretic. Everyone knows this. Why else would the church have incarcerated him? Madame Guyon, let me tell you the details of his incarceration. He is on a prison farm doing hard labor in the field from the beginning of the day to the end. He has already confessed to your immoralities. I have the power to grant you your freedom. I would hate to see a mother such as you also on a farm as forced labor. I understand that although a fallen woman, you are still a mother.

And a long day stretched out. I allowed myself the liberty of watching the floor so I could avoid seeing his taunting face.

"Do you call what you did spiritual? Traveling all over Europe like a vagabond?"

I felt a ray of strength fill my heart. Accompanied with my daughter and female friend, I remembered the snow-capped Alps, as white and glistening as my Lord. Memories of us laughing as we walked through a gorgeous mountain pass one time warmed me. Even in this prison, happy thoughts filled me.

I answered directly. "I traveled with my daughter and servants, not with Father La Combe. We occasionally met during these travels, but only in the company of others."

Four hours later, "Why did you keep Father La Combe's letters next to your bed?'

Sighing, I summoned my inner help. Maybe a different tactic. "We could save a lot of time if you would let me tell you what happened rather than accusing me over and over again of something I did not do."

La Reynie looked like I had slapped him—and as if he wanted to slap me in return.

Yet he persevered. "Father La Combe has already confessed."

Hour passed into hour. Then I tried again. "For the sake of your time, Monsieur. You are an important man, and I a woman with much time. Let me tell you what happened."

Chief of Police Reynie stood up, looking at the water torture machine they had used so successfully with La Voison. Yet his expression looked empty for a second and I wondered if he remembered the contorted look on the screaming woman's face as they continued to pump water into her overfilled stomach.

Turning back, he started with a different approach. "Do tell me of your life."

"First, Monsieur, let me tell you again that the name Family is not for me, but for my faithful servant who is also with me in these lodgings. Her name is Marie Delavau and we refer to her in love as Family. Yes, we are a family, a group bonded by the spirit of Christ."

I sensed his anger subside a little.

"For this, Monsieur, do you believe I should be burned at the stake?" And for a second I wanted to beg him not to commit me to the fire, as Bishop Bossuet asked, but then I knew that I should never plead. I should try to envelop him with the truth of what really happened and trust in the Lord.

After these eight-to-ten hour interrogations, I occasionally had a visitor, a priest from Fénelon's seminary, Joachim de la Chétardie. The first time he entered my cell he fell on his knees and began to pray. I looked at this fervent man, so spiritual and enraptured by the Spirit, kneeling in such a dense and hostile environment.

"I liked your book about prayer," he said to me at the first visit.

At the next visit, he spoke in a low voice to Marie, "You should not be in prison helping Madame Guyon. You do not deserve to be here."

I heard my faithful friend exclaim, "There is no other situation in Paris I want. My lady is worth more to me than that!"

I saw my situation clearly: If through my surrender to God I avoided faithless errors in the interrogations, I could still be condemned through remarks in my cell with this priest. He was a spy. There was no place to relax without dire consequences. And soon my danger intensified. Everything was designed to catch me off guard, and I, without counsel and in pain from my illnesses, watched them approach over and over again, waiting for the moment when I would break down and confess to crimes of which I was innocent.

The next day another interrogation began, and La Reynie continued pushing. "You need to explain why La Combe writes to you, 'The little church greets you, noble, persecuted lady.'"

Full of spiritual energy, I answered, "Paul says we are to greet one another in the bonds of the Holy Spirit." Even as I said this, I remembered the power of the love that embraced the small church in Geneva, and the unusual warmth we enjoyed as we became united one to another. Our lives had been transformed into ones of fiery love, and now in this interrogation, our Christian love was seen with deep contempt.

I paused and even in an interrogation could feel compassion for the head of the police. I ventured quietly. "Have you ever been part of such a church, Monsieur?" He stopped and no answer emerged.

"I wrote one of my books which later the church condemned after traveling on the Loire River. I wrote a book that I called *Spiritual Torrents*, in which I say this same river journey is like the one in which we seek God. We may get bogged down with possessions and merchandise like a heavy boat, but when we give our lives to God, we move quickly and passionately to God, like a running torrent.

And the river of our lives leads quickly to the ocean of God. When people come together on this same journey to God, a true and powerful church is created." I sat quietly. "Does that sound like heresy to you?" But he said nothing.

I shook off these happy memories and started. "Now, Monsieur, let me tell you the truth. When the sunlight hits the blue Lake Geneva and the river flows into this great lake with the blue of a sweet morning sky, our thoughts turn naturally to infinity. And the good Father La Combe dreamed big enough to create and build hospitals. We hoped for the fresh vigor of health for others. We wanted the same energy as our Loire River. And when we created these hospitals, the amazing pleasure of God surrounded us. This divine pleasure alone carried us with its powerful currents and torrents." Pausing, I emphasized. "The divine pleasure alone."

Feeling as if he were in a dream, La Reynie stood and left. Walking to his assistant, he spoke in an authoritative voice. "What foolish enterprise is this to arrest such a woman. She is innocent and speaks with the Spirit of God. We will not continue this injustice. Start orders to let Madame Guyon be freed. I think that even King Louis must agree with this."

Then in a loud voice, he accused the prison clerk, "You have tormented this person for so little."

La Reynie turned to me and in gentle words spoke to me. "All justice will be rendered to you."

I overheard this, but sadly I knew that this would not happen. The very power of the throne of Louis XIV wanted me condemned, and with Monsieur La Reynie's judgment of innocence, now I was in more trouble than ever with the French royalty.

Louis and Madame de Maintenon knew the importance of all their efforts and wasted no energy: Every look, every word, and every conversation contributed to their legacy. Maybe that was the gift of having worldly power. They had spoken against me and they wanted this supported by their legal system. But I knew that the Lord teaches us that every one of our hairs is counted, and so I persevered. If even my hairs were counted, I knew that the Lord cherished me in every one of my actions.

After hearing of La Reynie's judgment, Bishop Bossuet instructed the messenger. "Tell them at the Vincennes that La Reynie is not to talk to Guyon again. She has won him over and the news of this judgment could strengthen her heresies."

But a sympathetic guard made a surprise visit to my cell the next day.

"Monsieur la Reynie now understands that the powers of France are against you unfairly. I overheard La Reynie tell Desgrez, 'Let's get out of here. They want us to make that lady guilty and I find her very innocent. I do not want to serve as an instrument of her destruction.'"

I nodded and knew the truth of what the Spirit reveals. They tried to use la Reynie, but his moral righteousnes stopped this. I could see the truth of God in this chief of police.

The following morning an officer barked at me. "You will be leaving the Vincennes today for the nunnery at Vaugirard. Prepare to leave. You are a most fortunate woman to be leaving here."

I stood up with tears bursting from my eyes. "No, please, not this. Do not send me away from here. In Vaugirard there will be no witnesses to their torments and tortures. I have some protection here in this administration." I talked rapidly. "I beg you, talk to your superior. I do not wish to leave."

The soldiers merely stared at me. The younger one turned to the other soldier. "Have you ever seen anyone cry because they are leaving the dungeon?"

"No, boy. This is most amazing."

The soldier turned to me, "Has no one told you that you are to be set free?"

Shaking my head no, I quietly prayed, "Master Jesus, help me! Help me!"

A wall of light surrounded me and I knew that I was to resign myself to this action as it was allowed by the hand of the Lord.

I spoke again the words of Scripture from I Peter 5:6-7 that inspired my faith and actions. "Humble yourselves, therefore, under God's mighty hand, that he may lift you up in due time. Cast all your anxiety upon him, because he cares for you."

IX
At Vaugirard

Desgrez came to my cell the next day and I understood the significance that he himself showed up. If one was set free, they opened the doors and the person walked out. This state authority would take me to a new place of incarceration, and the Spirit testified to me inside that this place Vaugirard would be worse than the Vincennes.

I learned their plan. The state had taken two women and called them the Convent of St. Augustine. They placed them in a small, decrepit house outside of Paris. They had trained one of the women to watch me continually and convinced her that I was a demon. Any torments she heaped on me would be rewarded, in hopes that I would confess to whatever they wanted, and Madame de Maintenon would be justified in her complaints about me. In turn, this woman would receive money and a position if she succeeded in breaking me.

I was shown my cell, a small room in a dilapidated building, with boards hanging open on the foundation, so that I feared the building would fall in on me. A small door opened to a small garden where I would spend most of my time. A series of odd tests began, with my jailor keeping a list of what she claimed were my crimes.

This phony nun began to frame me with alleged crimes. She took my money and bought food and noted my extravagant eating habits. She ordered many newspapers to show that I was fascinated by things of the world. She accused me of having men climb into the garden and into my room. When the apricot tree in the garden fell down in a wind storm, she accused me of destroying it. I reacted to all of these ridiculous accusations with peace, and then she began to hit me regularly. Making a fist of her hand, she hit me on the face every day. With all of this heaped upon me, I prayed every day, "Let nothing separate me from the love of God who is in Jesus Christ!"

The cross of Jesus Christ sheltered me through all of this. To remind myself of this, I made three crosses and put them in the small garden next to my room. Because I knew that the cross of Jesus protected us, I wrote on a sign:

I go from cross to cross, and thus I spend my life!

To intensify these torments, la Chétardie came frequently, experimenting with new approaches to force a confession from me.

"We now have the evidence on you, Madame, and the crimes that you committed with Father La Combe. He has confessed and we have witnesses from Bretagne who will testify to your indiscretions with him."

Wearily, I responded. "But I have never been to Bretagne."

Without a word, he angrily stormed out.

Soon, the nun brought a workman to board up the only window I had so that I would be forced to live, cook and sleep in a room without ventilation. I asked the nun if I could speak to la Chétardie about this. Screaming, she grabbed my head with one hand and hit me on the face with her other hand.

I said, "I am known to people of honor."

While still hitting me, she yelled back, "Are you saying that I am not a person of honor?"

Quietly I said, "I will let la Chétardie know of your violent methods."

She threatened, "I do not recommend that. You will find yourself in deep trouble, and I know what I will do."

This was all unbearable. I never heard a word of comfort or consolation. Living in these inhumane conditions, I was constantly hit and tormented.

La Chétardie came to see me. I spoke forthrightly, "Just to live in a closed room is punishment enough, but to allow these insults and violence is unnecessary."

"You complain about nothing," he said. "All your friends have abandoned you and all you have left in the world is me. You should be grateful that the Archbishop of Paris got you out of the Vincennes."

"I would gladly return to the Vincennes where I was treated fairly. Here I am entirely isolated and can have no visitors."

"Nothing is wrong here. I want a letter written by you telling everyone how well you are being treated by me."

Realizing that for Christ alone I suffer, I trusted Christ to care for me and wrote the letter as he requested.

"No, no!" one of my servants cried out. "Madame Guyon is a saint."

"You are irascible and entirely mistaken," he said while walking quickly out of the door.

The nun worked at making the room increasingly uncomfortable: no ventilation, no light, and no foundation so that if I walked boards would fly up and hit my legs. My exhaustion increased and I became increasingly unable to even walk.

In my prayers I felt the presence of Jesus Christ and cried out to him, "Give me the grace to suffer everything for you! My only consolation, O God, is that You see inside hearts. All that I experience comes from your goodness to me."

My dreams became filled with both warnings and promises.

La Chétardie came to see me soon afterward.

He announced, "The Archbishop of Paris, Louis de Noailles, has proof of your guilt and you will never be set free."

With straightforward directness, I answered him, "Monsieur de La Reynie, the Paris Chief of Police, has found me innocent already. I owe it to God, to faith, to my family, and to me to request that you turn my case over to the Parliament where I would receive justice. I want my case removed from the jurisdiction of the church."

La Chétardie reluctantly answered, "I will speak to the archbishop about this. If Fénelon had not intervened, you would already be released."

Quickly, I responded, "If the archbishop has proof of my crimes, what difference is there if Fénelon is involved?"

"You should confess your crimes and ask God to have mercy on you. Before your time, other witches have received mercy, and you could have the same."

The torments continued. Because of my illnesses, I needed wine and the nun ordered an expensive wine and wrote it down in her book. As I drank some, it burned my mouth, tongue and burned all the way down my throat. A nurse asked a man to come inspect the wine and in fear, he announced that someone had put poison in it. It could not be drunk without death. For the following three weeks, I suffered great pain throughout my body and finally, after consuming large amounts of water, I found my health restored. To keep my equilibrium, I pretended not to know what was going on around me.

The nun said one day, "See! Guyon is so quiet; she has gone mad."

A nurse there to see me said, "This could also be patience."

"But see, her eyes are going blind also."

And it was true. Before, I could amuse myself by knitting, but now after illness, poisoning, and torments, my eyes seemed to be deteriorating also.

The nun came in one day. "Now that I have done my work with you, I have been made the Superior General of my order. Someone else will take my place."

I knew this promotion pleased her, and it was based on my suffering. The next nun was also warned about me, but had a conscience and seemed to suffer in this position. Quickly, though, everything began to escalate: I learned that my faithful servants were to be taken away.

The one Father la Combe and I called "Family" was the first to go. La Chétardie came to take her, and she said a tearful good-bye to me, as I lay limply in the bed. I said good-bye without hysterics.

La Chétardie complained, "Well now! Doesn't your patience ever end?"

I felt my spirit rising. "No, sir, and they will become exhausted from persecuting me before I have had enough of suffering."

Yet, I missed my faithful servants desperately. I never worried about them betraying me for a reward from the church, and now they were leaving through the force of La Chétardie. My unhappiness began to explode inside of me with the departure of these affectionate friends.

By now, I had endured about eighty interrogations, with the length of them ranging from eight-to-ten hours a time.

The new nun, having been at Vaugirard for only two months, came to speak to me and said she was leaving: her conscience will not let her participate in this.

I responded, "The worst is over though. Please, I beg you to stay. If you remain in this position, you will help me."

Her tormented expression supported the ominous words. "The worst is yet to come. I know horrible things will happen to you. I cannot be part of them."

And now I knew that extreme measures would be taken against me. Yet, returning to my cell, I hurt not for myself, but for those good and innocent people at Versailles whom they also were bringing down: Fénelon and the good dukes. I prayed, "O God, let everything fall on me. Let me be the scapegoat to take the sins upon myself. Do not let your saints become fodder for the birds of the heavens and the beasts of the field!"

La Chétardie brought in a new nun, who regarded me as a demon. Even with my resignation to God, such bad treatment and continual harassment made me very sad, yet I tried not to show this to them.

La Chétardie continued his plans: In the beginning of November 1697, he told me of another person of high standing who had signed documents testifying against me. Then La Chétardie brought in a document The Life of Mgr Jean d'Arenthon d'Alex written by the Bishop of Geneva, with allegations and stories about Father La Combe and me. My sadness grew as I understood how his accusations against me could be refuted easily, but no one would listen to me. They wanted me to say I was guilty so this could be said at Fénelon's trial in Rome. These leaders would stop at nothing to condemn Fénelon. The second nun was right: my time of testing was only beginning.

After twenty months in Vaugirard, a peasant who worked for one of the nuns decided to help me. This young woman came to see me one day.

"I can't believe what they are doing to you here. I told my confessor and he instructed me to help you. What can I do?"

No walls could keep out Jesus Christ, I thought to myself.

I gave her some money. "Help the poor when they come here looking for help."

"I will, but you know as well as I do, that they want to see you because you have healing powers."

Quietly I said, "Then bring them to me and I will pray."

The servant continued, "But what can I do to help you out of this unfair situation?"

Seeing her sincerity, I picked up a letter that La Chétardie had given me in which he wrote that everything he did, he did because of the authority of the archbishop of Paris. "Please take this to Archbishop Fénelon or at least someone who can get this to him. La Chétardie has written accusations in this letter, and at least one person outside of these walls will know what these church officials are doing and saying. In this letter La Chétardie admits that I have asked continually for judgment by Parliament. I want to be released from this church trial."

Without a word, she took the letter and walked to the door, and I gave thanks that the dark obscurity La Chétardie had cast upon me would be shattered even a little.

Later she came to see me again. "La Chétardie has been questioning me and asked me to say that you are a witch. I told him that I could only say good things about you. He started yelling at me, 'You are a stupid beast!' and after he lunged at me, I ran out of the room."

I picked up her hand and, holding it gently, thanked her for her help.

"But I am coming to tell you something else—my confessor said I must tell you. Yesterday I went into a room to clean and La Chétardie and another man were working on a desk. The other man was copying a document and La Chétardie said to him, 'No! He does not make his L's that way.' And then the man writing changed the words on his paper."

I waited while she gulped and took a breath.

"So I told my confessor last night and he said that it sounds like they are forging documents and I needed to tell you this."

La Chétardie desperately tried to find something to use against me. All he had was this evidence against me:

1. I read newspapers of all sorts that he had ordered for me.
2. I read fairy tales such as Griselda given to me by him.
3. I read novels, such as Don Quixote.
4. I ate green peas and drank wine mixed with quinine tonic as a medicine for my fever.
5. I had a parrot and a little dog to amuse my servants and me.

I hid my sad emotions as much as I possibly could, though sometimes in my grief I raised my voice and complained.

Then La Chétardie brought out all the power he had against me. One day the Archbishop of Paris, Louis Noailles, walked into my cell, dressed in full liturgical dress, as if prepared to enter the Cathedral for a church service. Following him was La Chétardie.

The archbishop sat and told us to sit. He took my hand and firmly placed my chair in the full light so he could witness all of my reactions to what he would say.

Noailles began with sweetness. "I have come to restore your relationship with this priest who says he does not want to serve as your confessor anymore."

I replied, "I have given him no reason for complaints and have confessed to him out of obedience." For my part, I could see this as only the grace of my Master Jesus: I confessed openly to this man dedicated to my destruction, but even though a bad priest, in the confessional his words testified to me about Jesus Christ and strengthened me.

The archbishop continued. "If you do not have him as your confessor, no one else will listen to your confession."

"The Jesuits will confess me!" I knew that with their love of mysticism, they would see my reverence to the great Teresa of Avila and would help me.

"You need to confess to me that you committed shameful and licentious acts with Father La Combe, and, because of this, you were in dissolution when you wrote your books."

"I did not do this."

"I will ruin you if you do not confess this."

"I have heard of your nephew's marriage to Madame de Maintenon's niece. Surely your happiness about this will overwhelm any desire to destroy me. But you can ruin me if you wish. Only what pleases God will ever happen to me."

"I am in despair when I hear you talk of God's will." The archbishop shook his head. "I have a letter here from Father La Combe confessing to these shameful acts with you." He took it out of his pocket and concealed the address on it with care. The handwriting appeared forged to me, although the forgery bore some resemblance to Father La Combe's handwriting.

"If the letter is from him," I told him, "Then let me confront him with it, sir. That is a good way to discover the truth."

La Chétardie jumped into the fray and said that cannot happen. "Father La Combe is deluded enough to think you a saint. We will not bring him into a trial."

"Then I will not speak either."

The archbishop was ready for that. "We will make you talk." I knew he was talking about words forced out by torture.

"No," I told him, "They can make me endure what they want, but nothing is capable of making me talk when I do not wish to do so."

He drew very close to me and whispered, "We will ruin you."

In a loud voice, I responded, "You have the power, sir, in your hands. You have all the prestige to do this, and I only have one life to lose."

"We do not want to take your life because all your friends would believe you a martyr. We must disabuse them of this notion. I order you to tell me when you had illicit relations with Father La Combe."

"I have had no sin with Father La Combe."

"I am your archbishop. I have the power to condemn you. Yes, I condemn you."

I smiled at this one. "Sir, I hope that God will be more indulgent and that he will not approve of this sentence."

"We will kill your servants, then, since they are deluded about you. Sign these papers confessing to sins."

"I will not act against my conscience and will not sign these papers because I would be signing falsehoods."

I asked to have the letter he had said was from Father La Combe, but he would not let me hold it. I saw the writing and knew it was a forgery: all the V's did not look like his.

"If Father La Combe wrote this letter saying we had sins between us, he must have gone mad in his sixteen years of incarceration."

And it was this forged letter that gave them the justification to send me to the Bastille, a letter so flimsy that if it had been in court, it would have been easy to prove a forgery. Now they perpetrated a fraud in France and in the Vatican as they attacked Fénelon by saying that he was friends with a guilty woman.

I knew the innocence of Father La Combe, and if his reputation was not cleared on earth, he would receive an eternal weight of glory in heaven for all of his innocent sufferings. Through my helpful peasant girl, I arranged to get a copy of this forged letter beyond the confines of the Vaugirard into the hands of my friend, the accused Archbishop Fénelon.

Three weeks later, Desgrez visited me. "The archbishop has accused you of a thousand crimes."

With my friend the peasant girl in the room, I asked him. "What have I done?"

The peasant girl jumped in the conversation. "She has done only good and not bad!"

I told Desgrez, "I told you when I came here that they brought me here only to make accusations against me. I do not fear the truth, only lies and allegations."

His eyes had tears and he whispered, "I pity you."

X
The Bastille

They took me to the Bastille.

The gray stones of the Bastille's tall imposing towers met my gaze. These were not the beautiful gray rocks of the Swiss Alps, but stones telling of raw human power to take my body into places of desolation. In this fortress of Louis XIV, I had no friends.

I knew the only intention at the Bastille was to make me confess, and I knew that they developed torture instruments here to perfect their interrogation method. My solitary confinement began in the Bastille. At the beginning I was put into an empty cell and had to sit on the floor; then the jailor Monsieur Junca loaned me a cot and a chair. Oddly enough, my first week in the Bastille was a time of happiness and contentment because I was alone with my Master Jesus.

Sadly the harassment began again. They chose a woman of social standing but without money to stay in my cell to keep me under continual surveillance. This caused me to be distracted from Master Jesus and I felt anguish over this, though I was not afraid of the surveillance. She hoped for a financial reward by finding out information about me, and so she intently watched me.

After a week my furniture and belongings arrived from Vaugirard. Among my belongings was a book by the Amsterdam artist, Otto van Veen, showing pictures of divine love with a depiction of the beautiful relationship between Jesus and our human spirit. I knew this book would sustain me wherever I went. When they catalogued my belongings, Junca listed this only as "Emblems of Love," so that it looked like I had pictures of human love. He refused to put the whole title and he told the Court I possessed abominable books.

Though at the beginning I felt the contentment of Jesus, illnesses seized me. The atmosphere in my cell was very humid, as there had been no fire there for a long time. I began to fall and lose consciousness and thought I would die. The confessor, Father Martineau, came in to listen to my confession but would not let me finish. Instead, he called for the Bastille doctor and asked him if I was going to die. The doctor said he thought not but that I could take a turn for the worse and die. Then Father Martineau told me, "I am only able to confess you if you are on the point of death." I then placed my fate in the hands of God and knew a true peace.

My servant "Family" (now incarcerated in a different prison) stitched together a bonnet for me. Desgrez decided to carry this to me and I received it with thankfulness. Yet, the woman spying on me took the bonnet, quickly unraveled the entire bonnet, and found a hidden note. My friend had penned in her own blood a loving note that read, "I will always be loyal to you, despite what they do to me." These were the extreme straits we had been reduced to, and yet Christ allowed this heart-felt message to get to me, a sick woman lying in prison.

Soon another reason I had been sent to the Bastille became clear. The new chief of police, René de Voyer Argenson, came to me in a state of fury, even before we met, because he was connected to those desiring my condemnation and death. La Reynie had been relieved of his position after his offer of justice to me.

Slam! "Come with us!" I left my cell.

I sat all day under the barrage of questions.

"When did you meet Father La Combe?"

I went through the usual dates feeling oddly sorry for this Judge d'Argenson who was so confused about life. How did it feel to work your whole life to end up asking ignorant questions such as these?

I felt like Christ asked me to treat this man with respect until the right day when I was to turn the table on him. Yet, how could I feel compassion for these people harming me, I wondered time and time again. Still the sensation of caring for them continued, and I watched them with concern for what they were doing to themselves.

"Tell me about your relationship with Father La Combe." At first I remained in silence and gave him no answer.

His anger grew and he exclaimed, "I have orders from King Louis to make you speak!"

I had always submitted to the king, so I began to answer his questions.

"Where did you live when you were fifteen?"

I was surprised at this question, but soon after my answer I saw that he had prepared a list of questions about my life from the time of my marriage to the present moment. This began an interrogation of eight hours about whom I had seen during my whole life. He also wanted details about any servant I had had and what had happened to them. Many of these details I either did not know or had forgotten. I felt afraid, and these interrogation sessions made me suffer in ways that I had never before: I feared not telling the truth and saw that with their choice of words, traps were constantly being set for me. I tried to cling to the idea that Argenson was only trying to reveal the truth and I should cooperate, yet his anger and shrewd questions showed me that he cared not for the truth, but only for my condemnation.

At one session, I ventured an idea that would save time. "All of my answers to these questions are in the records of the Vincennes. I have nothing to change from those interrogations."

"I will ask you the questions. I do not need to look at those phony documents that covered up the truth."

One day Argenson handed me letters that appeared to have been written in my hand describing encounters with La Combe. The forgery had been handled so well that even I could see little difference between my handwriting and the forgery. One particular letter described a short trip between Geneva and Thonon, a short trip I had done with a group of five or six people along with Father La Combe. I told Argenson the truth about this and he wrote in the court records, "She was alone with him in Geneva."

Argenson then showed me an order from King Louis reading, "No form of justice should be shown to Madame

Guyon." I read it and sadly wondered if it was a real order or not.

Through these forgeries and lies, I perceived Argenson's malice and bad faith. It appeared to me that the charges, never formally presented to me, were those of being a witch and having evil powers that killed babies. Argenson sent these ridiculous proofs of my witchcraft to both Louis' court and Fénelon's trial at the Vatican.

Then Argenson asked me questions directly about Fénelon.

"How many times did you see the Archbishop of Cambray?"

"I never went to his house. He came to see me by order of Bishop Bossuet."

Argenson wrote down that Fénelon came to see me but left off that it was the order of Bishop Bossuet. He said in anger, "I do not want you mentioning the name of Bishop Bossuet!"

I knew that I had to speak up. "Sir, a judge should not be so partial and should not show such anger against the persons that he is interrogating and show such devotion to the accusers."

His anger intensified, but he appeared shocked that I would say this to him.

That afternoon in my cell, workers came in and covered my fireplace with a wire net so that nothing could come down the tower.

"Why are you doing this?" I softly asked.

One worker turned to me and muttered, "They believe someone is throwing papers to you through the fireplace."

Truly I was not allowed to have fires in it, but this was laughable. I questioned, "Through such a high tower?"

No response. Later two guards came in and took everything apart in my cell, looking for any correspondence giving me legal advice and, of course, found nothing. The next morning the interrogations continued, beginning with ones about who was giving me legal advice.

"Sir, no one is telling me what to say, and surely since I am under constant surveillance, how could advice get to me? The towers are too high to throw small papers down into my cell."

Then in a derogatory fashion, he stated, "Then an angel dictates to you!" After that his interrogation style changed from an aggressive lion to a clever fox.

After the session, as the clerk gathered his papers together, he turned to me and whispered, "Poor lady, I feel so sorry for you!"

Trying to protect the clerk for his impetuous words, I answered loudly to Argenson, "I am telling you the truth about your questions." But I could see Argenson's furious look at the clerk and knew that he might have overheard the unfortunate clerk.

As Argenson could not penetrate into my thoughts, his anger grew, and malicious looks from him and Junca were all I saw anymore. I had no counsel but my own confident innocence that I had done nothing wrong. My interrogations with Argenson went on for three months, an amount of time not even allotted to dangerous criminals. After they ended, Argenson spent another two years investigating my life.

The woman spying on me had become out of control with her aggression and depression. After an interrogation,

I was being returned to my cell and found her tearing up my sheets. She had taken all my personal belongings, and I could tell no one and receive justice. Then she would sit and weep for hours, and in between sobs I heard her story. She had three children and a merchant from Paris wanted to marry her. They had told her she would attend a woman for a few days and make a fortune by doing so. Without asking her consent, they tore her away from her life and brought her to my cell where she spent time watching me. The authorities kept telling her, "The woman is a heretic and a witch! Find the evidence." She told them I did nothing wrong, that I prayed with sweetness and kindness. She could find nothing. Then they would take her away and convince her of my guilt. Returning her to my cell, she would at first be outraged and then depressed. The months away from her children and family were creeping by, and no wealthy marriage was in sight. She knew only her unhappy time with me in the Bastille.

Finally her distress in this sick environment made her ill and she had trouble breathing. I started attending to her and taking care of her physically.

When a guard brought our small meals, I begged for help. "Send a doctor! The young woman is dying. Or send a confessor to hear her before she dies."

The prison authorities knew that the words of a dying woman would carry a lot of weight in court, and instead of helping her, they began interrogating her.

"What does Guyon do in her cell?"

"She prays."

Angrily, they asked the same question and hinted at the answer they wanted. "Does she worship the devil in fiendish rituals?"

"No, she reads Scripture and the lives of the saints."

Even as sick as she was with her increasingly labored breathing, they returned her to my cell. Soon they carried the sick woman out of my cell and I never saw her again. Later they told me of her sad death. Argenson interrogated me a couple of days later. "She is ready to testify against you now about how you made the devil appear to her. She is telling us many things about you and your crimes."

With an intense frankness, I said to him, "She cannot do that. She is dead."

"How do you know?" was all I heard from him that day.

"When she was taken out of my room, she was having a brain seizure. Of course she is dead."

My life then became all torment. Angry malicious people surrounded me on all sides and I had no human contact or comfort. All of my natural vivacity died, but I now lived entirely in the Spirit. I felt the hand of the Lord over me and in the great oppression I suffered, though I now experienced only the life of Christ within.

Argenson and Junca did not give up their attempts to find evidence against me. Junca had a nineteen-year-old goddaughter whom he promised to marry if she could find something about me. Such a young and gullible age, he thought, this girl will find what I need. They brought her to my cell to live there.

Junca was connected to the Noailles family, that of the Archbishop of Paris, who offered to make Junca the governor of the Bastille if he found something against me. The interrogations continued nonstop.

The judgment from Rome about Archbishop Fénelon finally arrived. The Vatican gave a light sentence on his book Maxims. Monsieur Junca came to my cell.

"What will Archbishop Fénelon do?" he asked me. I was sure that Junca had been sent to question me.

"He will submit to the pope, for he is too honest to do otherwise," I answered in simplicity. And that was exactly what he did. They waited to see if I would say that Fénelon was treated unfairly, but I did not. I waited only for the justice of God.

The Vatican's Trial against Fénelon

Through some letters quietly brought to me, I learned what had happened in the Vatican with Fénelon's trial. The cardinals met, argued, and debated for two years. Father de la Chaise had rumors spread around the Vatican about the nature of the relationship between Fénelon and me.

The day in 1699 for the decision arrived. The results of this committee unfolded some dire news for Archbishop Fénelon. By a very narrow vote, the cardinals condemned twenty-three propositions of the *Maxims of the Saints* for emphasizing the passivity of the believer.

Pope Innocent XII sighed and ordered this written as a papal brief, not the higher condemnation of a papal bull.

Then the pope rose to the moment and said, "The Archbishop of Cambray erred through loving God too much; the Bishop of Meaux sinned through loving his neighbor too little." And so ended at the Vatican what is called The Great Conflict.

In the meantime Archbishop Fénelon stood fully vested, waiting to give his sermon at the Cathedral at Cambray. A messenger from the Vatican strode towards him. Their eyes met quietly. The messenger said in a soft voice, "The news is not good, Father. *Maxims of the Saints* has been condemned."

Fénelon stopped. Then bowing his head, "I accept the pope's decision. Please be my visitor at dinner following the Mass."

The messenger impulsively reached out to grab Fénelon's shoulder. "The Holy Father says you love God too much, Father. He has never said that about anyone else."

Fénelon's eyes filled as he started the long processional into the Cathedral, thanking God for His peace.

At the Bastille

They asked the girl watching me if I wept or threw tantrums.

"No," she said, "She prays and seems at peace."

When together, the girl and I talked. She leaned forward, her eyes flashing wildly. "He's going to marry me and I am going to be a real lady, not like you."

"No, he's not." I said. "Dear, this is a plot against both of us—he's going to use you and throw you away, yet use you as a way to destroy me."

I looked at the poor girl and wished to wrap my arms around her, as if she were my own daughter. But her haughtiness would have none of it. And I now saw my own disaster coming from every side.

Back at my cell, more concern surfaced.

"What an evening we had, madame!" the girl said as she went through my purse. She pocketed whatever money she found, yet I saw she was stealing from her own soul.

"Sexual sins aren't the only kind, dear," I answered, "but even these will destroy you."

The interrogations continued. Every day, only frowns and scowls, curses and yelling. Soon I noticed that I felt as if I deserved their contempt and hatred.

Now that the court case with Fénelon was finished, I sensed changes in the atmosphere surrounding me. Monsieur Junca came to see me and said, "Sometimes people are forced to do things that they do not want to do. You should write a letter of excuses to the Archbishop of Paris and ask him to come see you, and you will be released."

I knew this was a trap and that Archbishop Noailles would ask me to sign a condemnation of Fénelon.

"I have nothing to say to the Archbishop of Paris, and even less to say to you. It is quite useless for either of you to visit me because I do not want to leave prison. I find myself quite at ease in my solitude."

He appeared shocked.

"And I will sign no condemnation of Archbishop Fénelon. It is not up to women to condemn bishops: I leave that work to the pope."

Upstairs from my room was the cell of a prisoner, a priest, who paced continually and never paused for rest. His constant ravings led me to believe that he had lost his mind. In a place like this, despair was a constant companion. Without my Master Jesus I would not have survived the yelling, angry looks, malicious behavior, and unjust legal treatment with no counsel from anyone. They put out anything they want the public to know, and the harshness we endured destroyed many. There in the Bastille, you have no one. Outside the Bastille, you had lawyers to defend you and judges seeking the truth. Inside the Bastille you had only one judge who was also your accuser, who interrogated you as he wished, who wrote what he wanted from your responses, who dispensed all rules of justice, and afterwards no one sets it right. They tried to persuade you that you were guilty and made you believe they had many things as evidence against you. Wretched people who did not have the confidence that came from surrendering to Christ fell into despair.

There was only God's love, the abandonment to His will, and faithfulness to a suffering Jesus Christ. I counted this as an honor to be able to bear the same contempt that Jesus knew.

One day I heard the pacing stop upstairs and then heard him fall. I told the girl, "Listen when they bring him dinner. I think he has harmed himself." Later that day when the dinner was brought, I heard the guard yell out, "Go get a surgeon and Junca!" Never having seen him, I heard later that the prisoner had stabbed himself in the stomach and was drowning in his blood. The surgeon stitched him back together and he was well again in about ten months. Why they put so much energy into saving his life, when they were trying to destroy him through this incarceration was puzzling. The surgeon at the Bastille was very proud that the priest survived.

My crosses continued, but now I understood them. Through these crosses, God had delivered me out of many dangers. Through crosses, I had known the care of His Providence.

One night the girl watching me grew very ill. Her breathing became more shallow and lighter—panting really—and I saw her becoming weaker and weaker.

"Madame, help me!"

"I am praying for you." Then I ran to the door and yelled loudly, "The woman watching me is ill. You should get a doctor and come get her."

I heard no answer and the next day soon after she died, they came to get her lifeless body.

When I had an opportunity, I spoke to the governor of the Bastille.

"Please do not send me any more women to watch me. Even though they are young, they all die."

And that was the last one to live in my cell with me.

I had not heard from Argenson for two years, and then his interrogations began again, but now with a congenial Argenson who was clearly trying a different tactic with me. Now he brought in as a witness against me the man who stabbed himself and recovered. This man was a Catholic priest, although I never knew the charges against him. The priest had been trained to testify against me, and said that he knew me when I was at Thonon. Now through the questioning, it was clear for the first time what the charges were against me.

The interrogation began with a notebook of writings done by Father La Combe who wrote early in it, "O happy sin that has caused us such advantage!" Argenson acted like he finally had me with an admission of sin that happened between us. This was a laughable charge. I calmly pointed out that this was written by Thomas Aquinas and was the opening line of the Easter canticle. The sin Aquinas referred to was that of Adam and Eve which brought redemption through Jesus Christ.

Then they brought out the stabbed priest. He said that at our first meeting in Thonon, I was very cold to him. The next time I met him though, we had had an intimate conversation in which I spoke against the State, against Bishop Bossuet, and against my close friends at Versailles. The stabbed priest said I am a thief, an ungodly person, a blasphemer, and an immodest and cruel person. This line of questioning lasted for several interrogations with Argenson writing down in detail all of the priest's answers and ideas about me. After this testimony, Argenson said, "Ah! I am very satisfied with this interrogation. She has no refuge anymore or any evasion!"

These interrogations lasted for about forty days, and although I sensed God's grace to me, I was very upset and my interior life was torn apart. I could not eat or drink except a few liquids, but somehow the Lord's hand sustained me.

At the next interrogation what I said surprised me. I began with making sure of what the stabbed priest said. "So this witness said I was cold and unfriendly to him. Yet the next time I went into very confidential matters with him in a conversation that lasted one hour."

Gloating, Argenson agreed and handed me a transcript of the priest's testimony. I looked through it, although it was so long it would have taken hours to read.

Then I said, "How, sir, can a conversation one hour long, like the one he spoke of in his deposition, contain all that you say it did? You still have things you want to question me from a one hour conversation? This conversation would need to have been two days long."

Argenson saw his mistake but would not allow anything to be written in the court record.

I added, "Maybe he should add eight more hours to this alleged conversation."

Argenson understood the error, and although I could see he had pages of more questions, he picked up his papers and left.

I wondered if I had made a mistake with such a strong confrontation, though I believed that because of this last interrogation, at a clergy meeting in 1700, the archbishops declared that my morals were never an issue and I was innocent in this regard.

But after that my treatment became much worse. I only saw hideous faces. They treated me as a criminal. They confiscated many of the letters from my children and I burned the rest. I began to hope that they would take me to the scaffold so all of this would be over and I could go to be with my dear Master Jesus.

Argenson stated again the allegation that the priest had said I had lived with Father La Combe. I told him about my living arrangement in Thonon and, of course, we did not live together. I asked to talk to the priest whom I had never seen face-to-face. At the next interrogation, they brought him in and I did not recognize him. When I saw him, I asked him, "Sir, why do you accuse me of being a thief and other things?"

He said, "I did not say that."

I then addressed Argenson saying, "Please write it down in the court record that this priest has retracted his statements. I am going to appeal to Parliament and request that my case be brought to them. All of these interrogations have been useless!"

I had never seen an angrier person than Argenson. He yelled, "I will go to the King about this!"

I answered, "The King would allow me to defend my innocence because he is a fair person."

Argenson addressed the priest, "What did La Combe say about their happy sin together?"

The stabbed priest said, "Sir, that is the line from Aquinas that reads 'O happy sin'!"

Argenson said tersely, "You are a beast."

He turned back to me and I said, "All of this is useless! I request an appeal to Parliament."

Argenson said, "Do you want witnesses?"

Again, I repeated, "I want to go to Parliament. These accusations you make are all groundless."

The clerk of the court brought documents to sign after this interrogation. The trembling priest, pale as death, signed them and I did the same.

I waited for another scene.

Argenson stated, "You are tired of being in an honorable prison. If you want to taste the Conciergerie, you will taste it." If I wanted to taste torture was what he was saying.

As at other times, when they took me downstairs, they showed me the door and told me that it was there they torture. Then they showed me the dungeon.

I said, "It is very pretty. I could live well here."

The guard answered, "The water for the water torture comes in here." He pointed to the ceiling.

I told them, "Then we will place my bed right underneath there, along with a chair. I will be just fine."

The appeal to Parliament hit like a thunderbolt. I was left alone with my illness for the next year, and I saw I was in a situation of no justice. I felt compassion for this poor, wretched priest they had made lie about my situation. Now they no longer allowed the governor of the Bastille, Monsieur de Saint-Mars, to visit me, because he was sympathetic to my situation.

Now cracks began to appear in the formerly seamless attacks against me. One of the first came from Monsieur

Junca, who without warning visited my cell. He pronounced, "I owe my fortune to the Noailles family." I interpreted that as his way of asking my forgiveness for his attacks against me.

Then he added, "Your children should request your release."

I had, however, found a deep contentment in my cell and wanted to stay in this cross. I refused to request this, but one day my children came to my cell and I knew that the powers of the throne did not want me to be in the Bastille anymore. Later I heard that the Archbishop of Paris Noailles was so upset about my treatment he could not sleep. Political to the end, Noailles wanted me released but did not want to request this himself, because he would appear to have flip-flopped about me.

Odd as it sounded, now I did not want to leave the Bastille. I had abandoned my soul to Christ in this setting, and I tasted a divine calm. I sensed Christ's divine flame within me. This brought me great interior contentment.

Monsieur de Saint-Mars, the governor of the Bastille, came to my cell one day. "I hear that you want to stay here. I would be honored to offer you a permanent apartment here."

I stood up and offered him my hand. "I thank you from the bottom of my heart. Yet, though I would like to accept your offer, my Master Jesus wants me to serve him by leaving. He has work for me to do outside of the Bastille."

In the world's eyes, I had lived sick and alone in the Bastille for eight long years. In my eyes, though, I knew that the Lord Jesus lived with me and we shared joy as if we lived in a beautiful cabin in the mountains close to a river. His happiness carried me even in the depths of this horrific prison.

On March 24, 1703, four years after the condemnation of Fénelon's *Maxims of the Saints*, the heavy Bastille door opened and I was told that now at the age of fifty-five, Louis XIV did not consider me a threat anymore. I was picked up, placed on a litter, and was to be carried first to my son's house. I then moved to the town of Blois and lived close to my daughter. I was home again on the Loire River, in a town where Joan of Arc had actively worked to save France.

XI
Love's Crossing

My health failed during my decade-long incarceration in the Vincennes, Vaugirard, and the Bastille. I was fed only on small amounts of food, living in cold, torturous isolation.

They carried me lying limp in the litter and placed me down in a hall.

I was taken to a little home in Blois. My daughter walked slowly over to me with her tears bouncing everywhere. Anne-Marie knelt down and gently grasped my hand.

"Mama," she said very quietly.

Yet who was that leaning over me? I saw gray eyes wide with fear. Could that be my Anne-Marie?

And I heard and remembered all of the times I had heard "Mama" echoing through the dramatic pageant of my life. The memories awakened within me bringing forth my forgotten strength and long-ago joys.

Memories like "Mama, where are my dolls?"
"Mama, will we visit the sick today?"
"Mama, will you put my wedding veil on me?"

And now "Mama, what have they done to you?" And I focused my eyes for the first time on this distinguished woman, my Anne-Marie, an aristocratic Countess, and we wept and embraced. We were home together again.

At first I spent long days in bed, seeing no one.

I wondered, had the spiritual journey been worthwhile? Yet my heart still felt the fire of God. I yearned for complete union with Christ.

Then the letters started. My Anne-Marie carried the first one in, gently placing it next to me. I slowly reached for the letter and then I stopped, suddenly feeling vibrantly alive. The letter was from Fénelon!

My eyes overflowed. My defender, Fénelon courageously had written to me, knowing that even still the Sun King's wrath could descend on us.

Weakly I pulled myself up to a sitting position, noticing for the first time what an attractive room it was in which I lived.

I felt again the saving presence of Jesus telling me to write. Jesus accepted me, with all of my pains and all of the terrors I had known. These terrors were now written in my body and soul. I wrote in my diary, "How did my spiritual journey start? It began with fervent faith as a child, but then almost ended because of the family tensions. I sensed, though, that Christ was with me during those times of sorrow. And I sensed he reached out to me, offering me his nail-pierced hands as though we were fellow travelers in this world wracked by hatred.

"Looking at his hands, I loved him. I could only love him. I knew not why this suffering was allowed. I don't question that anymore. Christ's love was everything; His love was satisfying. And as I sensed this Son of Man who had borne the cross, I knew I was asked to step out of my life and go into the world offering my hand. When I offered my hand to God, I found humans everywhere suffering and in need of my ministry. People wanting to know: Is God real? Does God care?

I looked at people and could only smile and say, "Yes, my children, Christ cares and rules and loves immensely."

I realized, "In our sacrifice we become one with the Master Jesus. Our lives become a testimony to God."

A few weeks later, Anne-Marie entered my bedroom and leaning gently over, she started brushing and arranging my hair. "Mama, what sadness you have known! How do you understand this?"

I looked compassionately at my daughter; we had participated in sadness together.

"I used to wonder about who I was. A woman despised by many, but also a woman deeply loved by Christ. Anne-Marie, listen and find the mystery of Christ's love. What death will never rob from us is the interior path, the love of Christ within."

Anne-Marie listened quietly, stroking my gray hair, and finding peace.

I so wanted to tell her about the love of Christ. "I loved Him and I burnt with love because I loved Him. I loved Him in such a way that I could only love Him, but in loving Him I had no motive but Himself."

I knew the prophecy about my life had been fulfilled. My Anne-Marie was sheltered and loved in her family. My spiritual words of theology were being published all over Europe. My spiritual children flocked to my home to hear words of wisdom. I knew comfort in that all of my children, my hospitals, and my theology had found glorious, divine protection. The spiritual light protected and sheltered all of us.

I saw glimpses of the purified church in my home at Blois. Nonconformist Christians began to visit me, first a small stream of visitors trickling in, many Protestants from England and the New World, coming to see me. They wanted to know me, the woman who confronted the powers of Louis XIV and the court at Versailles, and overcame the challenges. An English aristocrat, Lord Deskford, became my secretary; and a Dutchman, Pierre Poiret, published all of my writings. Chevalier Ramsay worked for both Fénelon and me, and carried letters between us.

I knew that, with the Revocation of the Edict of Nantes, these meetings with Protestants could be punished with more incarceration. But now, as a part of the eternal body of Christ, I feared nothing. With my visitors, I happily wrote poems and letters that went around the globe.

One of my poems described my refreshed relationship with Christ,

I love you now with a new strength:
And without distraction,
My love is one hundred times stronger;
It is pure, simple and true.

And I told people over and over, "Abandon yourself to
God and find the real love of Christ within your spirit."

XII
Pure Love

I enjoyed life in my home in Blois. My visitors listened to me talk about Christ, and I found joy in knowing that the good news of Christ within our spirit would continue being shared with others.

My friend Chevalier Ramsay visited Fénelon in Cambray and told me what was happening in this historic town of Cambray. Throughout history the great empires—the Romans, the Franks, and the Hapsburgs— all desired this northern French town of Cambray because it was on a major trade route. In 1677, Louis XIV claimed Cambray as his own and waged many border wars there that had left this small town reeling with poverty and death. Louis had then banished Fénelon to be the Archbishop of Cambray and to stay there forever.

What had my exiled friend done in Cambray? He became Christ's ambassador to everyone he met. He gave last rites to dying peasants and carried food to starving families. He saw maimed and wounded soldiers all day long. Generals from any country welcomed Fénelon's help because they trusted him.

This town came to be defined by the presence of my friend, who could speak to you about the intricacies of the intellectual life in the French Academy or about where your Protestant relatives could find safety now that they were being hunted by the Sun King's armies. The residents lovingly called Fénelon the swan of Cambray, because this man acted with love. With ease, Fénelon traveled with equal grace through dark alleys and wide French promenades. The gracious Archbishop Fénelon understood human suffering because of his own overwhelming troubles and costly decisions made in the Great Conflict.

Fénelon continued his courageous writing. As a member of the prestigious French Academy, he wrote to them, "It is our insane and cruel vanity, and not the noble simplicity of the ancients, which needs to be corrected."

And what were the sounds erupting from the rectory of the Archbishop of Cambray? The town heard cows peacefully mooing, sheep bleating, and friendly dogs barking. They saw farm animals crowded into Fénelon's gardens. For when the War of Spanish Succession grew fierce, Fénelon saw his new ministry: Invite the peasants to stay with him. Preserve life and say yes to life! For he understood we were not only to preserve the life of human beings: save the life of the life-giving animals, the nourishing cows, the comforting sheep, the intelligent dogs.

One late afternoon the archbishop descended from his carriage after more pastoral rounds. Two multi-colored dogs ran over to sniff at his black cassock. Fénelon petted and asked, "How are you, my little buddies?"

Opening his front door, he saw in the hall of his residence a teenage girl dressed in a drab brown dress, cradling a young infant. Her husband sat next to her, his eyes glowing when he saw the older priest walking in.

"Archbishop, we can't thank you enough. It looks like the boy will live now."

Fénelon swallowed, pausing. Then he said softly, "I do not deserve this honor of the name you have chosen, but I accept this with gratitude." He caressed the infant's forehead. "How are you, young Fénelon? I look forward to your baptism this Sunday."

The husband shyly smiled, "There are other babies coming with your name. My son is just the first in a long chain of sons dedicated to you." He stopped. "Father, you have saved our lives and we will remember."

Moving slowly, Fénelon walked through the crowded hallways of people finding refuge in his rectory. He knew that his ministry to these poor had been successful.

The news we heard from Versailles was very troubling. In 1712, Fénelon's former student, the Duke of Burgundy, died unexpectedly. This young man, who was to be king, never had the chance to exercise his wisdom in leadership. We understood that France faced into a long history of uncertainty.

In faith we Christians continued our quiet work. We moved in the shadow of Christ, whose immense and eternal love supported, surrounded and upheld us all the days of our lives.

We moved in the shadow of Christ's love into unusual, unexpected places. Our music came from our fervent prayers, ecstatic praise, and committed love.

We moved in the shadow of Christ's love into the dark places of dungeons, ghettos, and unexplored places where human society tried to shut out His light; yet our intense vision of Christ never failed us.

We moved in the shadow of Christ's love: in the protected place of our heart where Jesus dwells telling us, I am the Way, the Truth, and the Life. The shadow of Christ's love announced, "God dwells with humanity!"

Christ's love brings a shadow of protection, a shadow of precipitating presence, a shadow of passion.

We carried the shadow of Christ's love to suffering humanity.

On June 9, 1717, I, now a sixty-nine year old woman, lay, as small as a young girl, long gray hair curling around my pillow: me, a woman who bore five children and countless spiritual children. I looked at my daughter Anne-Marie who gently caressed my head, and I saw I would soon move into a new world. I knew I would move towards the pure dazzling radiance of my beloved Christ. I looked forward to this oneness.

I learned so much through my life. Do you know what the world fears most? The world fears the passionate love of Christ. They tried to stop us from loving God and yet could not. The enormity of Christ's love shook the reign of Louis XIV.

Yes, the intrigues of Versailles and the Vatican converged and I suffered. But I also knew the glories of Christ's love; and once you know that, nothing else matters. My wisdom was Jesus, plain and simple. And when His plain and simple wisdom caused me all the troubles in the world, I would not leave Jesus.

And so, it was His love crossing into my life. Christ Jesus' love crossed through time and space, crossed through bars and horrors, crossed through long, desolate places of Vincennes and the Bastille to bring light to a desperate world. And I, Jeanne Guyon, give great thanks to Christ who brought the crossing of love into the world of Louis XIV and the court at Versailles.

Epilogue

Archbishop Fénelon died quietly on January 7, 1715, still banished from Versailles by King Louis XIV.

Louis died alone on August 10, 1715. The Duke of Burgundy whom Fénelon had tutored had already died in 1712. Because his son and grandson had already died, Louis was succeeded by his five-year-old great-grandson. On his death bed, he told the child to avoid war as far as possible, as Louis knew the pain caused by his many wars.

Jeanne Guyon died in 1717 in her daughter's home.

Madame de Maintenon died on April 15, 1719. At the time of the French Revolution, an angry mob dug up her bones and threw her remains in the street.

LIST OF MAJOR CHARACTERS

Miguel Molinos (1640-1696) Priest, spiritual director and author of books about the interior life. The Inquisition condemned his books in 1687. Molinos was arrested and incarcerated. Many historians believe that the Vatican authorities executed him.

Father La Combe: a celebrated preacher from the Barnabite Order, forced into hard labor and died in prison after 27 years.

Archbishop Fénelon: (1651-1715) Tutor for the Duke of Burgundy and spiritual director at Versailles. After Louis XIV banished him from the court, Fénelon lived in Cambray where he actively ministered to the poor and the soldiers.

Madame Jeanne Guyon: (1648-1717) Committed Christian and popular author who was incarcerated for nearly a decade.

Madame de Maintenon (1635-1719) Became nanny for Madame de Montespan and Louis XIV's children. She later married Louis XIV.

Chronology

1648 Madame Guyon born

1664 Marriage to Monsieur Guyon

1676 Her husband dies.

1681 Leaves her home in Montargis and goes to Geneva. Until 1686, she travels around Europe ministering to many people.

1685 Revocation of the Edict of Nantes which had assured Protestants' safety

1687 Father La Combe arrested

1688 Madame Guyon's first incarceration at the Convent of the Visitation. She is released from this incarceration through help of Madame de Maintenon. Guyon meets Fénelon the same year.

1689 Fénelon becomes tutor to Duke of Burgundy

1693 Guyon forbidden to teach at St. Cyr.

1693-1694. The Great Famine happens in which about 600,000 people starve to death.

1694-95 Issy conferences about her writings

December 27, 1695 Guyon arrested and taken to Vincennes

1697 Molinos dies in incarceration

1697 Fénelon publishes the Maxims of the Saints

1699 Pope Innocent XII condemns 23 propositions of Fénelon's writings.

1703 Guyon released from the Bastille; lived in Blois until her death in 1717

1715 Father La Combe and Archbishop Fénelon died the same year that King Louis XIV dies.

1717 Guyon dies

1719 Madame de Maintenon dies

Notes

1. Guyon, Jeanne. Autobiography, Volume 1. Translated by Thomas Taylor Allen. London: Kegan Paul, Trench, Trubner & Co., 1897. Pg. 65-66.

2. Guyon, Jeanne. A Short and Easy Method of Prayer. Translated by Nancy Carol James. Brewster, Massachusetts: Paraclete Press., 2011. Pg. 93

3. La Combe, Father. "A Short Letter of Introduction, Showing the Surest Way to Christian Perfection," published in .The Life of Lady Guion. Bristol: S. Farley, 1772. Pg. 301.

4. Guyon, Jeanne. The Soul, Lover of God. Lanham, Maryland: University Press of America, 2014. Pg. 69.

5. Fénelon , François. Letters of Love and Counsel. New York: Harcourt, Brace & World, 1964. Pg. 100

6. Fénelon "Letter of Fénelon to Louis XIV" (probably written in 1694) Letters of Love and Counsel, Selected and Translated by John McEwen. New York: Harcourt, Brace & World, Inc, 1964. Pg. 299-309

7. Molinos, Miguel. The Spiritual Guide Which disentangles the Soul, Michael de Molinos, Methuen & Co. LTD. London, 1950, pg. 160. (condemned in August 1687)

8. Bossuet, Jacques Benigne. Quakerism á-la-Mode or a History of Quietism. London: T. Martin, 1698. Pg. 16.

9. Guyon, Jeanne. Autobiography, Second volume. Pg. 96

Other Books by Nancy James Ph.D.

The Complete Madame Guyon
Bastille Witness: The Prison Autobiography of Madame Guyon
The Soul, Lover of God
The Pure Love of Madame Guyon:
The Great Conflict in King Louis XIV's Court

Gene Edwards writes on Jeanne Guyon

The Jeanne Guyon Nobody Knows

Other books by Jeanne Guyon

*Experiencing the Depths of Jesus Christ
Song of Songs
Intimacy With Christ
Final Steps in Christian Maturity
Spiritual Torrents
Commentaries:
Genesis
Exodus
Leviticus, Numbers & Deuteronomy
Judges
Jeremiah

---

*The largest selling book by Jeanne Guyon and one of the greatest
Christian classics of all time

Contact **SeedSowers Publishing House** for a catalog of these books and other books, including great classics from the past on the Deeper Christian Life, as well as new publications that will be appearing annually. Or go directly to our website and view the catalog online at www.seedsowers.com.

SeedSowers
Christian Books Publishing House
PO Box 3317
Jacksonville, FL 32206
1-800-228-2665
www.seedsowers.com